What the Cybernauts said about *The UK Internet Book...*

==

From: Stephen Soghoian <stephens@drjazz.demon.co.uk>
Subject: Review Copy of ur Book recd-Thanks
To: sue@s-sco.demon.co.uk
Date: Mon, 12 Sep 1994 01:24:02 +0100 (GMT+0100)

Hi There Sue

I just received a review copy of your new Addison Wesley UK Internet Book. I've read two chapters, it's very informative and user friendly. Perhaps I can write a brief review of it for the Internet alt.books.review newsgroup?

I think the book is very useful to NET users in the UK because it deals effectively with the nuts and bolts of how to get connected to UK internet providers, none of that material is covered by the plethora of American Internet books on the market.

Best of Luck with your new book. I hope it goes to the top of the charts for the Sunday Times Non-Fiction.

Cheers

–

Stephen Soghoian
American Journalist – London, England
reporter, "The American" Newspaper
stephens@drjazz.demon.co.uk

==

Date: Thu, 15 Sep 1994 11:11:23 +0000
To: sue@s-sco.demon.co.uk
From: Chris Davis <cdavis@smouse.demon.co.uk>
Subject: Magnum opus

Sue,
The herds of crocodiles snapping at my lower portions have prevented me from writing to you sooner to convey my delighted thanks for the UK Internet Book, which arrived a few days ago.

What a terrifically useful thing to have around: UK-based, plenty of Mac-oriented information, and very comprehensive stuff about Demon! The book has now taken up residence on my bedside table, and is consulted every morning and evening.

You have a really excellent writing style. I've always liked technical stuff written with an (apparent) grin – the spoonful of sugar to help the didacticism go down.

Best wishes,

Chris

==

Date: Sat, 08 Oct 1994 10:31:07 GMT
From: peter batty <batty@dedrum.demon.co.uk>
Reply-To: batty@dedrum.demon.co.uk
To: sue@s-sco.demon.co.uk
Subject: Hello

hello sue

A note to say thanks very much for the UK Internet Book. It encouraged me to take the plunge into this strange world and, most important of all, explained how! Brilliant!

Still completely fazed by it all (first logon yesterday), don't understand what I'm doing, but somehow have managed to get news (well, not "get" exactly – it seems to happen automatically), ftp some files, even seem to have got Cello up and running! (Did it really connect me to CERN and to somewhere-in-the-US-I've-forgotten-already at 02.30 this morning?)

All questions received by yours truly along the lines of "Wot's this Internet thing, then?" (yes, most of my friends are entirely at home in the Information Age) are now being answered with "Well, there's this really good book ..." and exhortations to BUY IT!

Sorry to trouble you with this inconsequential rambling, but in the book you did invite people to send you email. Regretting it yet? I would appreciate a reply of some sort, if only to discover that email actually works. The sad truth is – I don't know anyone else to ask :-)

peter batty

==

Date: Tue, 27 Sep 1994 10:47:48 +0000
To: sue@s-sco.demon.co.uk
From: Nicholas Wilson <njrw@njrwgsy.demon.co.uk>
Subject: The UK Internet Book

I have recently bought your book (yesterday evening). I have noticed that on pp. 138–139 you mention the "Summa" project. Could you tell me the address of the Summa project please. Thanks in advance. BTW, I like your book. Although I am only half way through (I read voraciously) I would have prefered it to Engst's ISK when I was trying to configure MacPPP and MacTCP.
Well done.

Regards

Nicholas Wilson
Guernsey

==

To: sue@s-sco.demon.co.uk
From: Hamzah <bnh@hamzah.demon.co.uk>
Subject: The UK Internet Book
Date: Fri, 6 Jan 1995 19:27:42 +0000

Great Book. I had to buy it in the end because I couldn't afford another 3 hours at Waterstones to finish reading it.

Why did I buy it for?. I wanted to set-up an account with Demon and was looking for a book for setting up the software etc. but in a way I was slightly disappointed. However, I managed to set up Trumpet Winsock using the Appendix in your book. Great I thought, I should be able to set up my mail now. Alas, I realised this is not the book for those sort of instructions.

I also did want to find out about what the Internet does, the technical bits and pieces, and where to go etc. Your book is great for this. I am not what you call a 'Guru' but I did learn a lot.

So on balance I would say it was well worth the money.

BTW (see I learnt something!), I did not get to use the free month sub from Demon because I enrolled before I got your book. Never mind!!

Keep up the good work.

Cheers

Hamzah

==

Date: Fri, 23 Sep 1994 23:14:21 +0700
To: sue@s-sco.demon.co.uk
From: Robert Firmin <bob@bljswap.demon.co.uk>
Subject: Getting Started with MACS

I bought a copy of your book yesterday, which I am enjoying very much. It's a nice change to read a book about the Internet from an English angle.

I got my package from demon, including the software and the Internet Starter Kit. I successfully loaded the software, which for me was nearly a miracle, not being computer minded.

Regards from Bob Firmin

==

Sue
I've just got back to work after my holiday to discover "The UK Internet Book" on my desk. Very nice indeed.

Mike

—

Michael Bernardi   mike@childsoc.demon.co.uk

==

Date: Mon, 02 Jan 95 18:00:13 GMT
From: Louise Morse <louise@morsepts.demon.co.uk>
Organization: The Morse Partnership
To: sue@s-sco.demon.co.uk
Subject: The UK Internet Book.

Dear Sue,
Read your book – still reading it and I think it's brilliant. Don't understand it all, but hopefully, getting there. Only been connected 3/4 days and at the moment have more questions than answers. Probably everyone else flies it the moment they're connected, but I'm still getting my head round the software.

Question 1: have you written other books? Titles, ISBN's?

Question 2: is there a kind of local news pin-board for Cambridgeshire?

Happy new year.

Louise Morse
The Morse Partnership
louise@morsepts.demon.co.uk

==

Date: Wed, 21 Sep 94 19:33 BST-1
From: Peter Reid <preid@cix.compulink.co.uk>
Subject: the uk internet book
To: sue@s-sco.demon.co.uk

Just bought your book today, it looks excellent so far, I must have browsed my way through about half of it! It is about time we all insisted on proper UK sourced books on the Internet instead of filling the pockets of all these Americans.

best wishes
peter

==

Date: Wed, 2 Sep 92 12:54:07 GMT
Organization:
From: Bill Lockley <block@faqer.demon.co.uk>
To: Sue@s-sco.demon.co.uk
Subject: UK Internet Book

Enjoyed your book immensely, also your sense of humour! Given the implementation problems I had, I don't know what I would have done without your book. Hope you make lots of money.

Best regard and thanks,

Bill lockley.

[One of your (hopefully +ve) stock replies would do fine.]

==

The Daily Telegraph

GUIDE TO THE INTERNET

SUE SCHOFIELD

electronic Telegraph

ADDISON-WESLEY PUBLISHING COMPANY

WOKINGHAM, ENGLAND • READING, MASSACHUSETTS • MENLO PARK, CALIFORNIA • NEW YORK
DON MILLS, ONTARIO • AMSTERDAM • BONN • SYDNEY • SINGAPORE
TOKYO • MADRID • SAN JUAN • MILAN • PARIS • MEXICO CITY • SEOUL • TAIPEI

Cover designed by Designers & Partners of Oxford
and printed by The Oxted Colour Press Ltd, Oxted, Surrey.
Text designed by Sally Grover.
Cartoons by Martyn Jones.
Typeset by Wyvern Typesetting Ltd.
Printed in Great Britain at the University Press, Cambridge.

First edition (*The UK Internet Book*) published 1994. Reprinted 1994 and 1995.
Revised edition published 1995. Reprinted 1995.
This edition adapted from *The UK Internet Book* printed 1995.

ISBN 0-201-87747-3

British Library Cataloguing in Publication Data
A catalogue record for this book is available from the British Library.

This is the single most useful tool – apart from your computer – in getting up and running on the Internet, and once you are there, in learning how to get the best out of it. Sue Schofield has brought together all the information which you need, and provides up to date contact details. What is more, this is not a US or 'international' book full of American phone numbers. Buy it, read it, and keep it with you. It will save you a lot of time and tears.

Howard Oakley, 'MacAgony' columnist in *The Mac* magazine, describing the first edition of Sue Schofield's *The UK Internet Book*

Electronic Telegraph Starter Pack Special Offer

Connection to the Internet for only £15.00

Electronic Telegraph and Demon Internet can connect you to the Internet with a special Electronic Telegraph Starter Pack for only £15.00 (normally £25.00), plus £15.00 plus VAT per month for unlimited Internet access.

Electronic Telegraph is an electronic newspaper, based on *The Daily Telegraph*, which contains specifically edited news, City stories, sport and features.

By clicking on a headline, users can call up full stories including colour photographs and graphics.

An archive facility is also available so that users can read articles that they may have missed.

Electronic Telegraph is currently available to all users of the Internet; it is published each weekday morning on the World Wide Web (WWW) via servers from Sun Microsystems. The Telegraph has licensed a stable, advanced version of Netscape™ software to enable easy access and navigation for users. Electronic Telegraph is available on PC and Macintosh platforms.

Electronic Telegraph Starter Pack

For £15.00 (a discount of £10.00 on the normal price) you will receive **connection to the Internet via Demon Internet – the most extensive dial-up Internet access network in the UK – Netscape plug-and-play software on disk, a user-friendly manual and your own Internet site and email address.**

Thereafter, a subscription to the Internet via Demon Internet (offering unlimited access) will cost £15.00 plus VAT per month. The only additional cost to users is the telephone charge to a Demon Internet Point of Presence.

You will need a computer and a modem; the special software provided in the Electronic Telegraph Starter Pack allows users to connect directly to the Electronic Telegraph Home page. The standard dial-up service provides a direct connection to the Internet, a full read–write Usenet news feed, multiple mail addresses (POP3), unlimited on-line time and no volume usage charges.

Simply fill in the application form that appears within this book. Alternatively, for more information write to Electronic Telegraph, Demon Internet Ltd, Gateway House, 322 Regents Park Road, Finchley, London N3 2QQ or telephone: 0181 371 1200/fax: 0181 371 1201.

The Telegraph plc and Demon Internet Ltd reserve the right to withdraw this offer at any time and to refuse any application.

Preface

Computer technology is on everyone's consciousness. You can't go into a bar without hearing talk of it, your kids are immersed in it, the Man On the Clapham Omnibus reads computer books on the way there – and back again, and Lollipop Ladies go home to their laptops and modems at the end of the working day.

The heart of this revolution is the simple notion that people and computers benefit from being connected together to form small groups. Here ideas can be exchanged, battles can be fought and philosophies propounded. Other small groups can be wired in too, until larger internetworks are formed and suddenly thirty-five million people in the world – more than the population of Belgium – are sending messages, browsing files, and generally interacting with each other over the Internet. The Datasphere is all around us, and the only limit to jumping on to it is a willingness to grapple with the sometimes awkward technology.

The impact the Digital Revolution is having on businesses and individuals is enormous. Where Evelyn Waugh's William Boot was despatched to Ishmaelia with a typewriter and a cleft stick, today's journalists have metamorphosed into cyborgs equipped with mobile phones, personal computers and modems. And where John Bull once depended on the postman for his correspondence, he now checks his electronic mailbox twice a day to pick up the mail, delivered in hours instead of days by the global computer network.

It has to be said that there are a few flies in this electronic vision of Heaven (or is it Hell?). Today's Internet is not the Information Superhighway of Senator Al Gore's dreams but a relatively slow B-road, heading towards something much larger and faster, which hasn't yet been invented. Moreover, much of the Digital Dirt-track is coned off to the average cyber-motorist, mainly because of the tedious rates of technological progress by UK telecomms companies, and the high rates they charge us for the privilege of keeping in touch by modem. Today's computer technology is also by and large hostile, unless, like me, you make a small living from telling computer newbies how wonderful it all is. But these caveats should not keep you from your modem. The Internet is the best free communications medium we have – in fact it's the only free communications medium we have, and its place in business and recreation throughout the Western World is already fully established.

The Electronic Telegraph (ET) service was conceived in mid-1994, not as a ground-breaking method of selling exotic computers to Telegraph readers but as a way of providing information to the growing army of people to whom information technology is a way of life. These people are managers in companies, scientists, management consultants, and the polite and perfumed ladies who work in banks and building societies. Tomorrow's emailers will be the milkman, the schoolteacher and anyone who is fortunate enough to have a job. A year ago the Telegraph's venture into electronic publishing was seen as a revolution, today access to the World Wide Web and to electronic mail is seen as not only commonplace, but vital to the economic and intellectual growth of the economy and to individuals.

The ET service brings you three things: ease of set-up with licensed software, largely due to a lot of behind the scenes work within the Telegraph's IT department, full access to the Internet and its many sources of information through the World Wide Web, and a joyous toy called Eudora POP3 mail, which, when you've got the hang of the thing, will let you call your electronic mailbox from any Internet terminal in the world. It will also provide the basis for enhanced use of the vast Internet correspondence lists (Listservs), all of which use email as the transmission medium.

Much of this book discusses Internet technology – because you can't become part of the information revolution without a grasp of whatever it is that everyone else is talking about – although the book is mainly jargon free. It describes the multitude of other services available on the Internet, including Archie and Veronica (named after characters in the American cartoon which perpetrated the Sixties hit 'Sugar Sugar'), Gopher, FTP and such like. References to Mosaic, the World Wide Web browser, should now be taken to refer to Netscape. The version of Netscape you get with your ET account is unique, and carefully tailored to the UK ET service for ease of set-up. (If only it had been as easy as this in the Early Days, a year ago....)

Once you're up and running you might sit down with a mug full of your favourite recreational chemical and browse through the book. You'll emerge at the end in possession of enough techno-babble to get a job on the Telegraph's Innovations page, or at least to hold your own with the average 15-year-old on the subject of computer communications.

Oh – you'll also be connected to the Internet.

The rest is up to you.

Bon voyage.

Sue Schofield
sue@s-sco.demon.co.uk
June 1995

For Tatz, who made it,
and Black Woolly, who didn't.

Contents

Technology is a queer thing. It brings you great gifts with one hand, and stabs you in the back with the other.

C.P. Snow

Part I

Internet basics

1 Internet basics

'Internet providers have started to spring out of the ground like worms on a damp day...'

In the beginning there was the cold war, the Kennedy administration, and the Defense Department, spelt with an 's'. Out of that came the Internet as we know it, a sprawling network of networks, spiralling around the world like a thing spiralling around the world. There are connections to it in almost every country of the world, there are no charges for using it, and no limitations on the amount of data you can take from it, or copy from it. At the moment the Internet is the greatest free knowledge base on the planet, with the emphasis on the words 'at the moment'.

It's a bit of a mystery why the Internet has taken so long to reach the consciousness of the UK computer-owning public. And why the sudden interest now? Perhaps it's the rapid increase in the ownership of cheap computers, or is it the fact that Internet providers have started to spring out of the ground like worms on a damp day? Whatever the reason, the Internet is this year's flavour of the month, to mix an already poor metaphor, and this book hopes to get you set up along with the other 20 million people who are already plugged into the thing. It's rumoured that Internet connections are selling at the rate of two per second, so don't be surprised if you find that things are a tad busy, once you get there.

What you need

All you need to hook into the Internet is a telephone modem or an Ethernet cable which ties in with an 'Internet provider' (IP). At the basic level you might just have a simple mail connection via a bulletin board, at the top level you might have full access via a suite of software on your computer which knows about something called TCP/IP. (Don't worry about the jargon – yet.) This latter method is a bit different from the sort of computer based communications you might be used to. If you have a CompuServe or other dial-up bulletin board account you'll be familiar with terms like 'downloading', 'file transfers' and ASCII, which will provide a good grounding for using the Internet. But as you'll see, the Internet interacts with the user's computer in a different way to almost anything else you've come across, and you'll need a guiding hand in the early days while you're still fighting with impenetrable jargon

Computers can communicate with each other over bits of wire. That's the simple bit. The complicated bit is getting the hang of the Internet by picking up some of the technical jargon that surrounds it. This is because the Internet is a heap of computers which use a particular set of utilities and programs to communicate with each other, and occasionally with human beings. As things stand at the moment, the computers on the Internet have the upper hand, and you can't just plug yourself into a socket on the wall and get going, which you can do with almost every other consumer product. So you can deduce from this that the Internet isn't yet a consumer product, although it will be in a couple of years' time. And because it's not a consumer product, you, dear reader, have to fight with the impenetrable language of the computer-geek or the UNIX Dweeb, but not for long.

It should be said early on that users do not have to get involved with any of the technicalities of hooking up to the Internet, because there are any number of commercial companies who will come along and connect you up in exchange for a brown envelope full of fivers. But many of the UK people on the Internet have chosen to get involved with TCP/IP software because they like mucking about with computers. However, it's possible for non-technical users to get hooked up, as we are about to see.

Starting out

Let's start at the beginning. The first thing you need for access to the Internet is an Internet access account. It takes the form of provision of an access point to the 'Net, and generally speaking, you'll pick up that node – or permission to use it – from an Internet provider (IP in the jargon). These people supply connections to the Internet in the same way as a telecomms provider supplies a telephone service, and there are a growing number of them in the UK.

If you're a student, or an employee of a large company, you might already have an Internet connection available to you – as your educational body or employer will have registered a block of addresses with the Internet authorities. In that case you just need permission to use the node, which will generally appear to the user as a number, such as 158.152.24.106. The number is the 'address' of the computer on the Internet, and it's assigned to the TCP/IP software on the machine for the same purpose as a telephone number is assigned to a telephone. Once the address has been assigned, the computer becomes a 'network node' which can then access a TCP/IP network locally via Ethernet or LocalTalk cable. A TCP/IP network is a bunch of computers hooked together with cable (or modems or radio waves) using the TCP/IP protocols, which are explained in the next chapter. So a network, for the purposes of this book, is two or more computers which can exchange data with each other and an internetwork is a heap of networks connected to other networks, so that all computers on all the individual networks can exchange data over the large interconnecting network.

It's possible to access the Internet via a modem, but remember that when this happens the user is actually logged into a distant computer, not directly to something called the 'Internet'. It's the remote machine which has the connection to the Internet, not the modem.

Terminal and network connections

Commercial Internet accounts come in several flavours. The only 'real' type is a fully fledged 'network' connection, where your machine at home or in the office becomes a TCP/IP 'client' on a network. 'Client' means that your personal computer is half of a transaction based system – your client needs to see a 'server' at the other end before it can be used. This can happen over a direct Ethernet or modem connection – and a network connection will normally give you full access to all the Internet services such as file transfer with FTP, Usenet, Internet Relay Chat and so on. You will also get the benefit of a full Internet machine name (like ***s-sco.demon.co.uk***) and a user ID (***sue***@s-sco.demon.co.uk). Benefits include being able to use the vast range of TCP/IP software, and files transferred to your machine will actually arrive directly on your hard disk.

This isn't the case with a 'terminal' connection. A terminal connection means that you access someone else's Internet computer on a network, usually via a modem. You lose the client–server model (explained in Chapter 3) you'd get on a full network connection, so you can't use TCP/IP software for access.

A terminal connection won't give you a machine name either, but it might give you an Internet mail address. And it won't let you download files direct to your hard disk because terminal connections have to take the files to the remote server and store them in a mailbox area, from where you later download them. (The CIX bulletin board service is a good example of a terminal connection provider.) To get over the problems of users sitting on phone lines downloading files once to the server and then again to the remote machine, some terminal services have introduced a facility called Batch FTP. It gets the files while the user is logged off, for collection at a later time.

There's one other major hassle with terminal connections – not being able to use all that fancy TCP/IP based software with them. Mac and Windows users have software available which graphically displays the directory tree of a remote server, or the

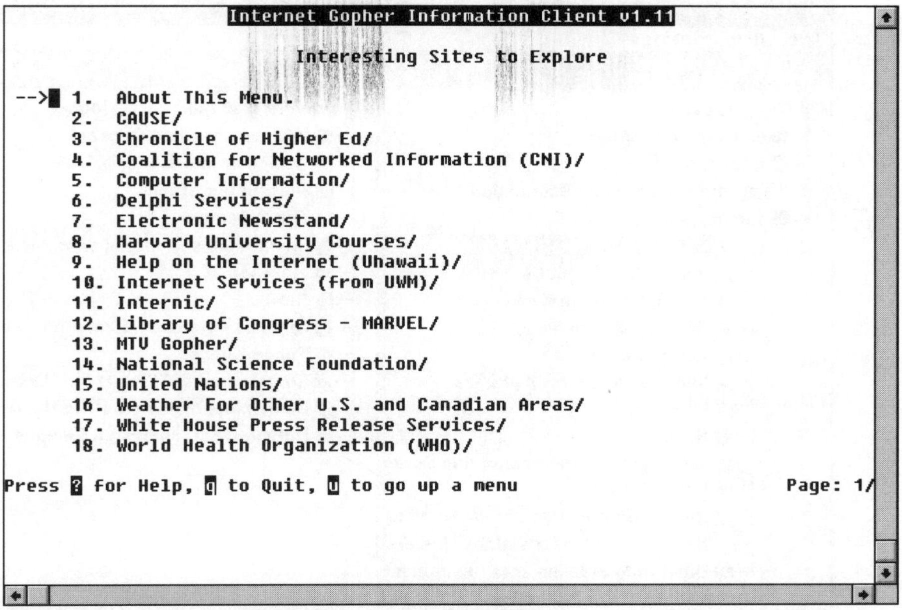

Figure 1.1 *Terminal based services can't run TCP/IP based software. This is the view of Gopher through a terminal service.*

result of a Gopher search. A full network connection allows these users to navigate around the Internet with mouse clicks and pretty pictures, and consequently they curse terminal connections which don't allow this to happen.

Because the Internet is so popular many dial-up bulletin boards are implementing terminal connections – so you should be aware of the differences before you part with money. The real feather in the cap of the network connection is that TCP/IP allows multitasking. You can use as much of the available modem or Ethernet bandwidth as you can grab and that means with a fast modem you can send and receive mail while grabbing files from a remote site. Each task you run is called a 'session' and it's common to have multiple sessions open in various windows. Multitasking saves money, or at least it does if you have a personal computer and software capable of doing it.

To sum up – **terminal connections** give you email in and out, some file transfer and telnet facilities. A **network connection** gives you full file transfers, a real machine address

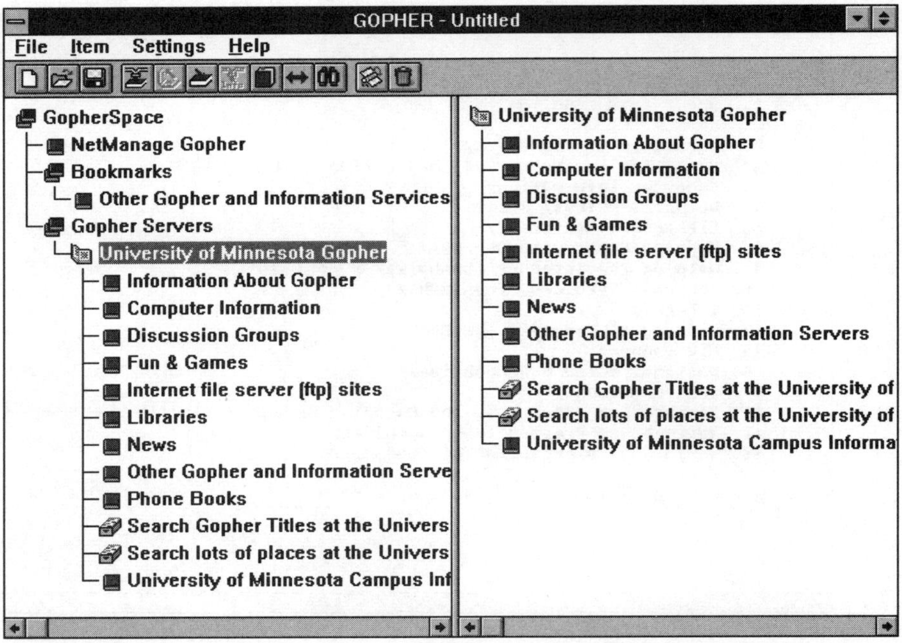

Figure 1.2 Windows Gopher client running with TCP/IP. Navigation is faster and easier than with a terminal service.

(often with multiple user access), and it lets you use TCP/IP based programs.

So – it's make-your-mind-up time. If you only need an electronic mail address then a terminal account with one of the providers already mentioned might meet your needs. On the other hand a full Internet connection brings a lot more functionality – although it's only going to be of real value if you use it – or have the software to exploit it. But think for a moment. Most of the next five years' development in information transfer is going to occur on the Internet. You'll get international voice transfer for the price of a local phone call, the ability to mail multimedia documents (sound and vision) around the world, and eventually, communications such as video on demand, video phone calls and much more. Oh, and there's even something called the Information Superhighway around the corner, but no one yet has decided what it is. If you want to be part of this revolution then go for a full Internet account now. You'll pay less per megabyte of information transferred over a full Internet connection than you will over a terminal service, and you'll be ready for whatever the Internet decides to chuck at you in the next couple of years. You'll also save yourself the nuisance of changing your email address once you do decide to change.

If you are a Windows user, or a Mac user or an Amiga or Archimedes user then it's recommended that you go straight for the throat with a full network account. You'll be able to use all of the wonderful graphical software coming onto the Internet. But if you are a DOS user then things aren't quite so clear-cut. Most of your interaction with the Internet will be via character based terminal emulation and you might find that terminal services are sufficient. But think carefully before you sign up – are you always going to be using DOS? Do you only want occasional Internet mail? Will you be content with a character based command line interface when you see things like the World Wide Web running in full sound and colour over a phone line? If you can unequivocally say yes to these questions then a terminal account may be sufficient, but if you've got any hesitation at all then go for a full network account.

Access points

The other major consideration before you sign up is the relative geographical distance between your location and the Internet provider's access points. These are called Points of Presence (PoPs) which is geek-speak for 'telephone number'. Many of the major Internet providers only have direct dial-up access to London based numbers. This means that users outside London will be paying a fortune in phone charges for access. Some providers make access available to distant subscribers over the packet switch network – but you'll pay extra charges if you use this, and you won't get anything like the full throughput that the latest modems are capable of. Moral – if you live outside London look for a provider with a PoP near you. (If you travel around as part of your job, then look for multiple PoPs.) And don't pay packet switch charges unless you are absolutely sure it's the cheapest option. Remember that file and information transfer takes longer over packet switch than it does over dial-up lines, and it costs more because you have to pay packet switch charges – even if these are reverse-charged to your provider's account, as they often are.

Pricing

The service providers all have different ideas about what constitutes fair pricing. In general you should try to avoid paying hourly charges in addition to phone charges, because the Internet encourages browsing and you'll end up with large bills, especially in the early days when you're finding your way around. Watch out also for fees levied on the amount of data or mail transferred through your account. Look for a provider who charges a single fixed fee for access. It's not recommended that you pay by the minute for access, unless you want to see your service provider get rich, in direct inverse proportion to you getting poor. Charging rates will depend on whether you are using a modem (dial-up) account or whether you want a full-blown corporate installation, but in general you should only pay for rental of the IP address – not for the amount of data you pump through it, or the amount of time you spend using it.

Since this book was first published, many suppliers of terminal based dial-up services have started to advertise their offerings as 'full Internet connections'. This is potentially misleading, or at best ambiguous.

A full Internet service is generally taken to mean one where TCP/IP software is used to provide the connection via TCP/IP access. Readers should therefore be careful about making this distinction – one reader mailed me with a woeful tale of how he'd bought TCP/IP browser software for his terminal account only to find it wouldn't work. For the purposes of definition in this book, services such as CIX, CompuServe, and Delphi offer terminal accounts, not full TCP/IP access, and TCP/IP software will not work with these services at this time.

Summary

The difference between a terminal connection and 'full' network access is large:

Terminal-only access means that:

- You *can* send and receive text mail, and you do get an Internet-savvy mail address.
- You *can* often use Gopher, telnet, FTP and other utilities on your host system to transfer files and log on to remote computers, but you're dependent on the facilities offered by your host service.
- You *cannot* receive files directly to your hard disk – you have to download them from the host, once the host has received them by FTP.
- You *cannot* easily attach binary files to mail messages to users outside your host system, unless your host has compatible 'front end' mail handling software.
- You *cannot* easily extract binary files from mail messages from users outside your host system, unless your host has compatible 'front end' mail handling software.
- You *cannot* easily run multiple sessions on your computer – which means that you can't send mail while you're transferring a file

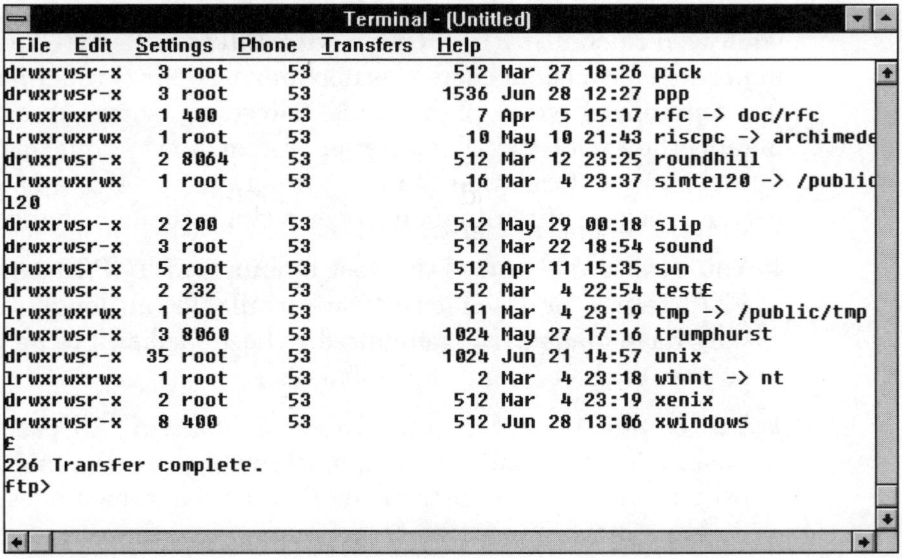

Figure 1.3 *An FTP server screen from a terminal service.*

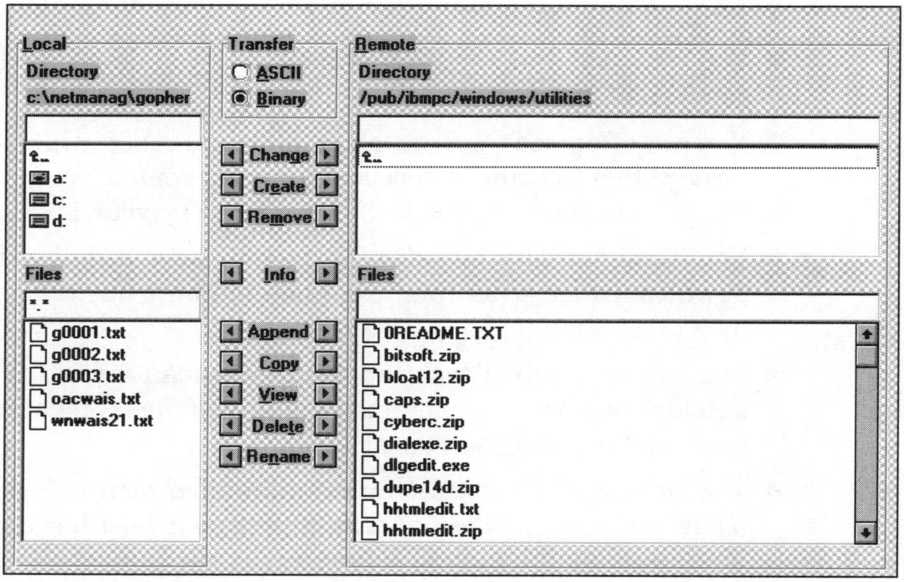

Figure 1.4 *Windows FTP client. Files can be dragged from the remote service to the local hard disk or viewed automatically with Write.*

while you're chatting to a friend with Internet Relay Chat. This is important for modem users – as maximizing your throughput is vital for minimizing your phone bills. However, some Mac systems, notably the First Class client–server system, now permit this, and the CompuServe Information Manager programs for Mac and Windows permit a degree of multitasking over a single modem connection.

- You *cannot* use any of the vast amounts of TCP/IP based mail, FTP, telnet, or Usenet software available (although your host may have made arrangements for these facilities to be provided as part of their 'front end' software.)
- You *cannot* have your own Internet 'domain'. In practice this means that you can't set up a machine of your own and let other people log on to it to transfer files or leave messages. This is perhaps more important to business users than to recreational users – but it can be useful sometimes if you've left a file on your home or work system and you are somewhere else.

Network access means that:

- You *can* receive files directly to your hard disk.
- You *can* easily attach binary files to mail messages to Internet users.
- You *can* easily extract binary files from mail messages from Internet users.
- You *can* run multiple sessions on your computer, thus saving money.
- You *can* use any of the vast amounts of TCP/IP based mail, FTP, telnet, or Usenet software available.
- You *can* have your own Internet 'domain'.

Cons for full network connections:

- You'll have to configure TCP/IP and dial-up software to run on your computer. It's not always easy...

2 Software for Internet use

'There's a huge amount of Shareware available...'

You need a fair amount of computer technology to get started on the Internet. However, almost any personal computer can be used to access the 'Net – as long as it has various bits of Internet-savvy software available for it.

Regardless of computer type you'll need:

- **TCP/IP software**. This provides the basic transport mechanism which handles your data over the 'Net. There are various types, from various sources, but without it you'll have no full access to the 'Net.

  You must have TCP/IP software, unless you're running a terminal account.

- **SLIP or PPP** if you're using a modem. These are the 'drivers' which allow TCP/IP to work over serial lines. It's SLIP or PPP which handles the modem dialling and hang-up, as well as providing a text file (called a 'script') which you use to automate the login procedure.

  You must have SLIP or PPP software or Windows 'Socket'-type software to access the Internet over a modem, unless you're running a terminal account.

If you have a UNIX machine you'll find that most of the software you need to communicate with the Internet is probably already built in.

Software supplies

You get hold of TCP/IP, SLIP or PPP as *software programs*. It's unlikely that your High Street Washing Machine and Colour Telly supplier will know what you mean when you say you want a Gopher

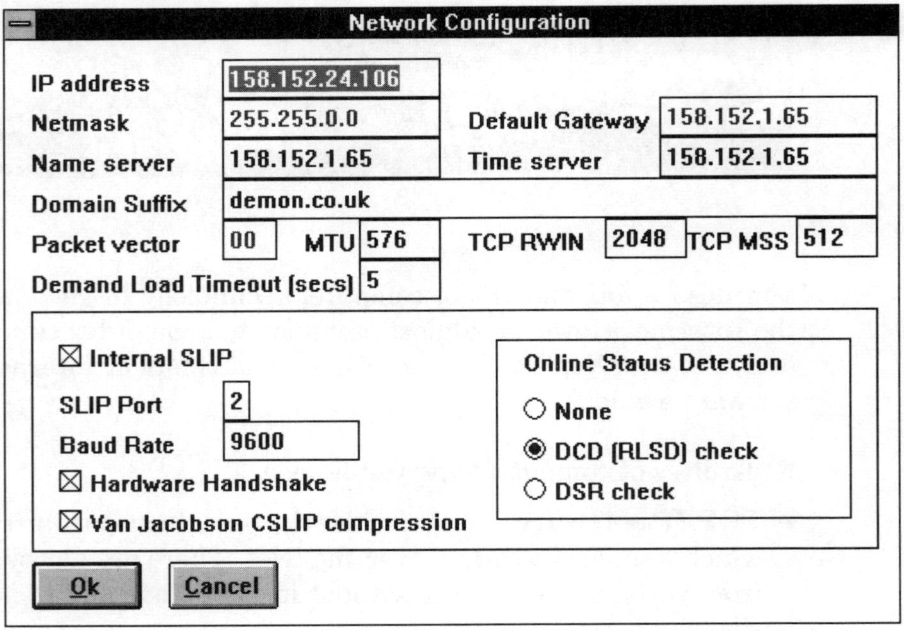

Figure 2.1 *The TCP/IP configuration in Trumpet Winsock for Windows. You need TCP to hook fully up to the Internet.*

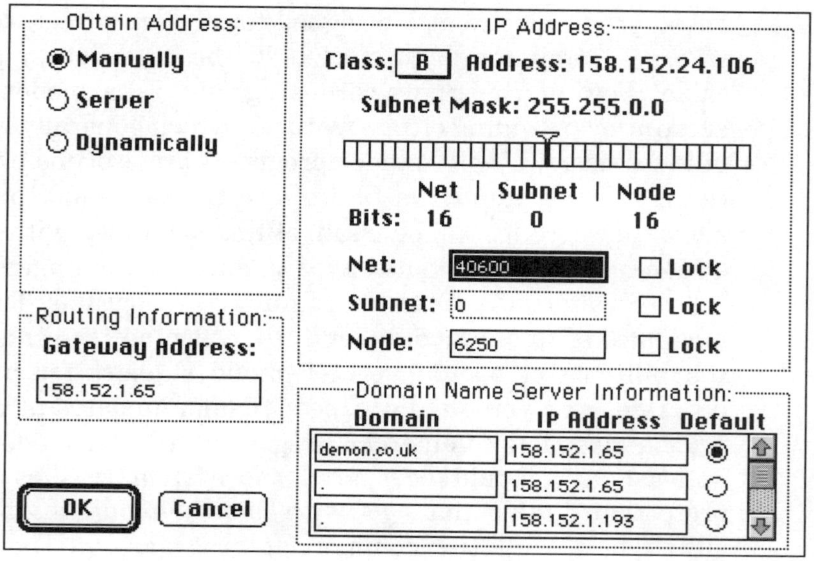

Figure 2.2 *Mac TCP configuration screen. It's very similar to the TCP/IP set-ups for Windows.*

client with SLIP and TCP/IP, so as things stand you will probably rely on an Internet provider to send you the requisite programs. If you already have an account on one of the dial-up systems somewhere, you can often download the programs for free, and of course the Internet itself has dozens of programs available for most computer types. But the most difficult problem for newcomers is getting hold of the software, a problem which will ease as more commercial programs come onto the market.

Shareware or commercial?

You should decide at the outset whether you want to use Shareware programs, or many of the free Public Domain programs available on the Internet. These programs are cheap or free, tend to offer good functionality and are in use on tens of thousands of computers. The downside is that updates and support are sporadic, the programs are not tailored to the services provided by your Internet provider, and there's no guarantee that one program will work alongside another during a multiple session. Most of the Shareware TCP/IP based programs are also designed for use on 'direct' connections – where a computer is connected to the Internet by an Ethernet cable. Few of the Shareware programs take modem users into account by providing offline features, which generally means higher bills for users. Usenet reader programs are a prime example – you can count the number of Shareware Usenet reader programs that allow newsgroups to be read offline (that is, with the modem disconnected and the data saved to disk) on the fingers of one foot.

The alternative is to use commercial programs. These cost real amounts of money, but tend to offer better integration and reliability. You should get telephone support for a commercial program, and you should expect regular updates at a reasonable price. Again, few commercial programs cater for modem users, but at least you should be spared the system crashes and general protection faults that go with using handfuls of Shareware, although not all the commercial programs on the market are perfect. At the moment there are few decent commercial programs that offer good levels of integration for users, although many more will appear on the market as suppliers begin to realize that the Internet isn't a one-day wonder.

Application and client software

Once you have the basic TCP/IP and SLIP or PPP software, you'll need application software to access the various corners of the Internet. For FTP you'll need *FTP software*, for email you'll need *email software* and so on. These are the **client** applications that let you hook into the various application servers you'll find on the Internet. These programs communicate through the TCP/IP link, which is operating through your modem, which is being managed by SLIP or PPP. Does that make sense? You choose client software just as you would choose a word processor or other computer application, that is, you listen to what all the experts tell you, and then go and buy the same program as the guy next door has. In some cases there are no commercial programs available, and you'll have to use the freeware or Shareware options, but once again, it's early days for the Internet in the UK, and there will be more Internet-compliant software available as time passes.

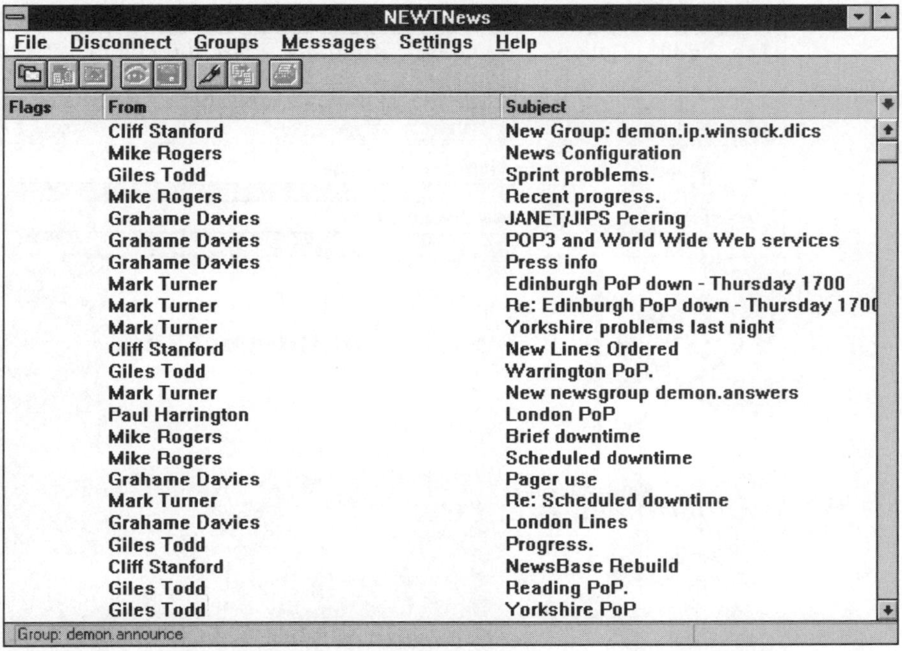

Figure 2.3 *NewtNews, part of Internet Chameleon. It's commercial software, and should therefore be expected to run without problems.*

In practice you will probably end up using the Shareware software distributed by your provider, or by the guy next door, unless you're a business that can afford the services of a consultant or dealer. Early generations of Shareware programs for the Internet were slightly lacking in many respects, but have improved drastically over the last year. There was also a flood of updated software for WAIS, Gopher and the World Wide Web in 1994 and it's now possible to get going for very little outlay.

It's important to remember that whatever software you end up using will be out of date in months rather than years, because the Internet is growing and changing at a phenomenal rate. The basics, SLIP, PPP and telnet, will remain the same, but the other services are evolving rapidly. This may influence your decision as to whether you'll use Shareware or commercial software to get going with the Internet.

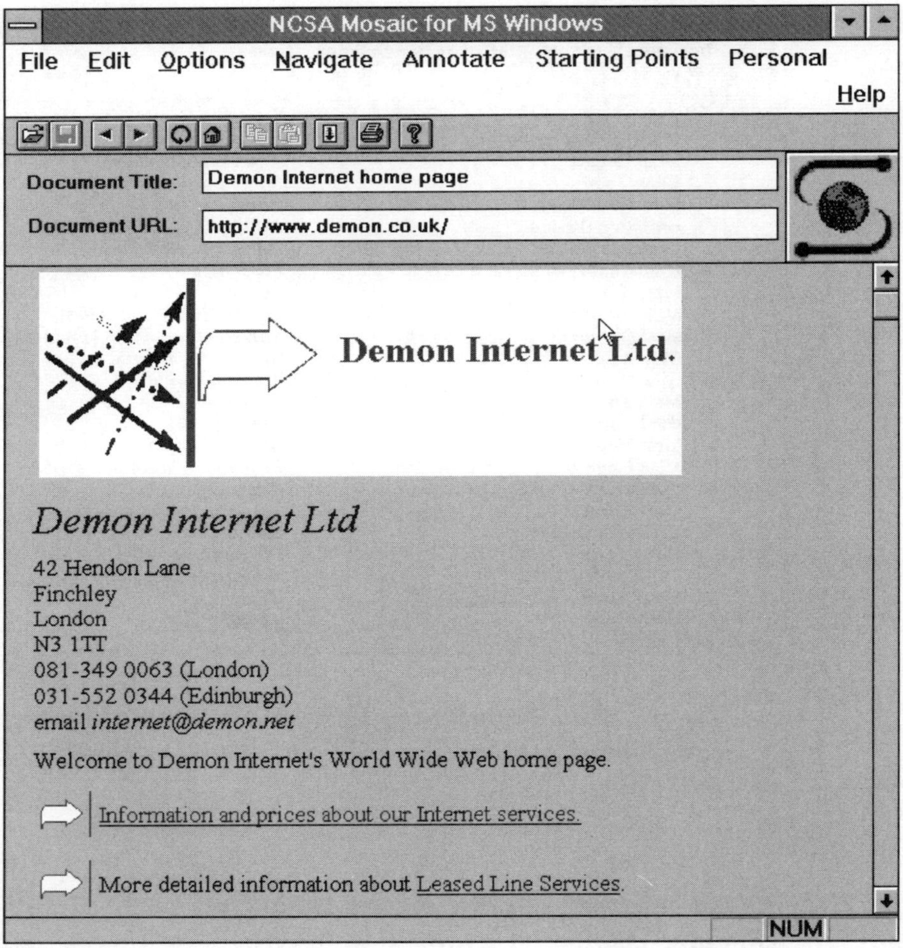

Figure 2.4 *The spectacular NCSA Mosaic client software. Early versions were prone to hangups on some systems.*

Shareware or commercial ware?

The Internet works as a community of sorts, and as it's a computer-centric community many of its denizens are computer programmers or code-dabblers. Consequently there's a huge amount of Shareware on the 'Net, and not a little of it aimed at TCP/IP users. There are two sides to Shareware. On the one hand there's the noble concept of publishing low-cost software which may be of use to others, on the other hand there's the downside of buggy code, untested software and zero support.

A lot of first-generation Shareware falls into the latter category. If it's version 1.0 then it's often full of bugs. But there are exceptions. Some of the Shareware programs offer great functionality and few bugs, so you may want to use them, and this is where the problems start. Much of the Shareware on the Internet originates in the USA, and is aimed at Ethernet users. US Shareware people seem in the main to be based at some educational establishment with a permanent Internet connection thrown in. That's the reason why you don't get many Shareware mail programs with SLIP dialers attached to them or Usenet readers that dump the data to hard disk.

You'll also find it hard to register your favourite American Shareware program, because many of the authors have moved on from their last known email address, or because your bank wants to charge you 25 dollars to raise a registration cheque for half that amount. Getting support or receipts from US Shareware authors is difficult too, and there are few UK corporate accounts departments who will raise a cheque without seeing a pro forma invoice. So in many cases Shareware authors cut their own throats by handling the administration side of their business inefficiently, and UK users are stuck with the dilemma of using unregistered software.

At the moment there is little you can do about this, unless the Shareware author takes credit card orders by mail or fax. Many of them don't because of the huge levies charged on small companies by the credit card authorities. Some Shareware can be registered via CompuServe's SWREG service, but then you need a CompuServe account to use the facility.

But do you need to use Shareware products to get onto the Internet? In most cases the answer is 'yes' unless you are prepared to fork out the large sums required for commercial software. VersaTerm and Internet Chameleon – the two packages used in the preparation of this book – cost around £150.00 each by the time delivery and VAT are taken into account, so you can see why the low-cost Shareware option is so attractive. Alas, if you use Shareware without paying for it for any of the reasons above then you are depriving the author of income, which might just be funding the next whizzo release of your favourite email or News program. Probably the only answer is to lobby your Internet

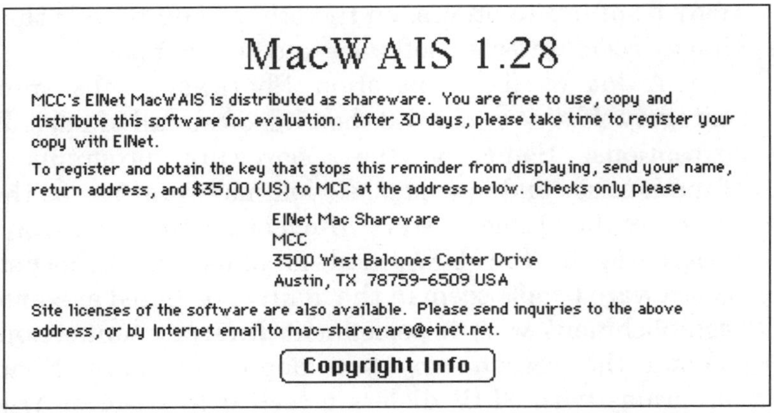

Figure 2.5 *Shareware registration screen from MacWais. Most UK corporates are not prepared to use Shareware.*

provider to arrange for site-licensing of the Shareware products with the author(s). This is easier to do *en masse*, and the provider can then license the software to users. But until that happens you are morally obliged to pay your Shareware fees wherever possible, even if the author makes that difficult for UK and European users.

Finally, you may find that you have to use a kludge of ill-matched software to provide the suite of TCP/IP programs you'll need to make use of all the Internet facilities. This is fine in the UNIX world, but not so good for Mac and Windows users where kludges often mean system crashes when two programs are used simultaneously. But it's early days for Internet software for personal computers, and if you are patient you will find more low-priced good software is being written for PCs, Amigas and Macs. When that happens prices of commercial software will fall, giving the user more real choice. Already larger providers such as British Telecom and Cityscape are designing their own access software for the Internet, and it won't be long before providers who offer only Shareware software will start to lose out, especially when easy-to-use custom software becomes freely available. The start of this awakening is already here – Apple have included the MacTCP control panel with the latest release of System 7.5 and Microsoft Window's '95 will include TCP/IP networking too. 1995 will see a large explosion in the number of TCP/IP based software packages available in the UK, and the revised NetManage Chameleon for

Windows is a good example of the way software is evolving to meet market demands.

Watch out too for Internet provision from some unlikely people. Microsoft are about to launch their own global service, with the software to match embedded into Microsoft applications such as Word and Excel. BT, the BBC, IBM and other large organizations are already jumping on the bandwagon and the Internet will be repackaged and sold as a boxed product in high street stores by Christmas 1995. Look out for offers from the national papers as they resell Internet provision to tie in with their own World Wide Web pages...

3 Internet technicalities

'You won't become a Network Guru by reading this chapter...'

You don't need to read this chapter if you've got all your Internet software up and running and you can get your mail, send messages to 20 million other people, and fight with all the other Internet services you've got at your disposal. You only need to read it if you want a brief indication of how the Network of Networks works, and what all the fuss about TCP/IP is about. This is only the most basic of primers – if you need more information, or are saving up for a beard and sandals so you can become a Network Guru, then you'll find all you need on the 'Net itself – or in your local bookstore. This chapter just points you at some of the buzzwords. You won't become a Network Guru by reading it.

How it all hangs together

Computers on the Internet use something called the Internet Protocol to pass messages around over cables, fibre optic links, or bits of virtual damp string. 'Internet Protocol' is abbreviated to IP for the sake of brevity, and a protocol, in this sense, is a series of conventions that describe how data gets chucked around between computers. IP is a 'packetizing protocol' – that is, it chops data up into small chunks, adds the address of the intended recipient and the address of the sender, and hopes that's enough information for the packet to get to its destination, or back to the sender if it doesn't. The packets are re-assembled (or not) when they get to the destination, to re-create the original data. The actual bit of wire – the connection between the sending computer and the destination – isn't really a bit of wire, but a virtual link which might go over any number of fibre optic cables, satellite links, packet switch networks, dial-up phone lines with modems or whatever comes to hand.

Smart boxes of electronics are used to pass packets between connected networks. **Routers** are boxes that connect different sorts of physical networks together. You might hook up your office Ethernet cable to a router so that the router can convert the Ethernet stuff for use with a modem over a phone link. At the other end you'd have a router and a modem doing the reconversion from phone line signals to Ethernet signals. A **bridge** is a similarly smart box that joins or bridges two similar or dissimilar networks but makes the connection invisible to the user. If you wanted to hook up your network to the one in the next office you'd use a bridge. Bridges are smart enough to work out which computer on the Ethernet should get which packets, but not smart enough to hook straight into modems, which is the job of the router.

Confused? The main thing to remember about all of this is that it doesn't need to be remembered – because if ever you have to fight with a router or a bridge to get your Internet connection going you have a serious problem. But it's handy to know what the techies are talking about when they mention *routing problems*. Most domestic users will never need to get involved to this level – and most commercial users will have a guy with a degree in Altered Consciousness (the Network Guru) to sort all of this out.

All this stuff about routers and bridges is a diversion – IP packets leave one computer and if all's well eventually reach their destination. But IP doesn't always deliver stuff in the right order, or at the same time. Packets arrive depending on all sorts of variables, like the amount of traffic on the net, the amount of network routing that's available, the number of maintenance staff on holiday, and so on. To make some sort of order out of this possible chaos virtually all Internet computers now use a second protocol to control IP. Transmission Control Protocol (abbreviated to TCP) is the controlling protocol which ensures that packets arrive in the order in which they were sent. In fact the use of TCP over an IP link looks for all the world like a direct point-to-point link, although TCP adds a considerable amount of overhead to IP packets. Despite this it's the TCP/IP *pair* of protocols which make the Internet work.

TCP/IP

It's all very well to go around bleating about Internet and Transmission Control Protocols, but you will be saying 'Well heck, this doesn't get me very far'. In fact TCP/IP won't get you very far at all, unless you have a network to talk to, and for most of us that means either using that piece of Ethernet cable you found lying about under the desk, or hooking up to the 'Net via a modem. Out of the two, using a modem is by the far the more difficult, as modems are not designed for use by human beings. And in both cases your TCP/IP software will need to be configured – which means feeding it with the address of the network and workstation, and information about which transport mechanism you're using. Modem users will also need either SLIP or PPP software. These provide methods of getting TCP/IP to work over a serial link, which is what a modem is.

The setting up of a machine for use on the Internet will be done for you in a commercial or university environment – but at home you're on your own. You have to fight with the setting up of TCP/IP, the dialer software in your implementation of SLIP or PPP, and the setting up of addressing and other server based information. This takes about a morning if you've done it before, or a day if you haven't, so allow plenty of time. In TCP/IP no one can hear you scream.

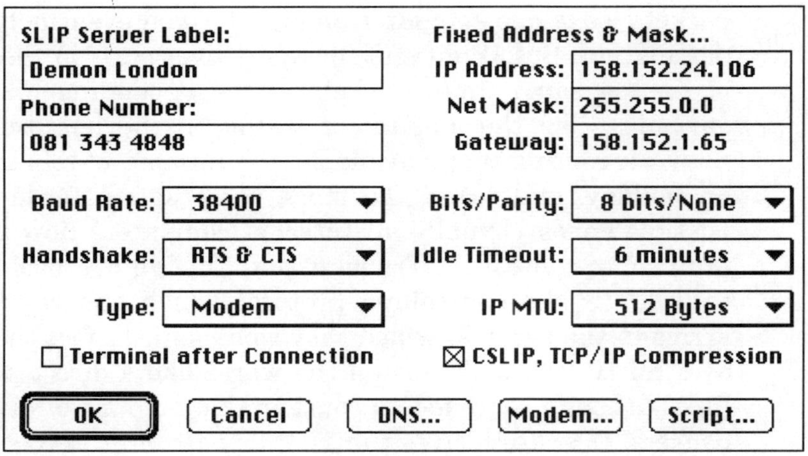

Figure 3.1 *Typical SLIP set-up from VersaTerm. The IP address is allocated by the Internet provider, as is the gateway address.*

Many a SLIP

Modems were not designed specifically for use with TCP/IP, and to get your Mark Four Whizzbang Wonder to work with it you are going to need either the Serial Line Interface Protocol (SLIP) or the Point-to-Point Protocol (PPP). You buy these as software utilities, or get them for free from the Internet or your Internet provider. Both of these, as far as the user is concerned, sit on top of TCP/IP and make it work over the serial dial-up link that exists while your modem is behaving itself. SLIP and PPP handle things like the telephone number of the service you are calling, the address of the computer at the client end of the link (yours) and whether or not to use compression over the link. Quite often these programs will pick up the address of the remote computer from the TCP/IP controller software you've already installed.

If you are already familiar with standard computer communications programs for personal computers then some of the basic operations of SLIP and PPP might seem familiar to you. With SLIP or PPP managing the TCP/IP link between you and the remote network you don't have to worry about things like downloading

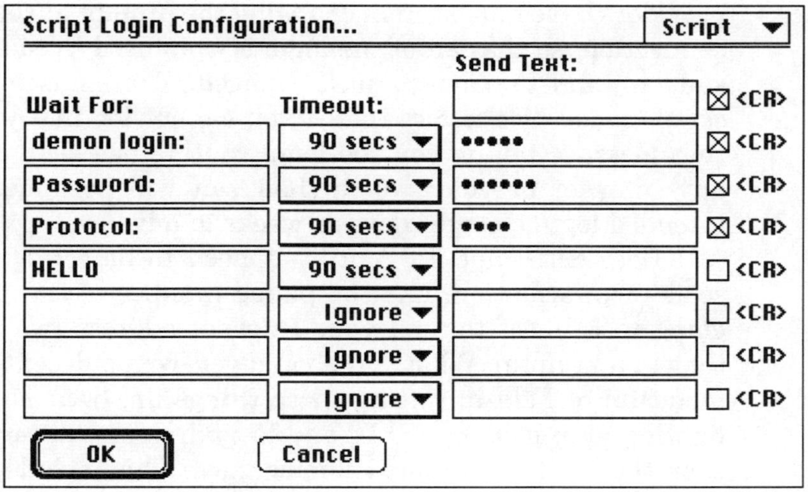

Figure 3.2 *Login script for SLIP. A carriage return (CR) is sent at the end of each line if the box is checked.*

files, but you still have to deal with novelties such as parity, handshaking and setting up IP addresses.

Comms geeks will argue the toss about the merits of using SLIP or PPP but to a large extent it depends what your Internet provider has decided to offer you. No PPP? Use SLIP. No SLIP? Use PPP. It's that simple, unless you want to make it difficult. To an extent you'll find that the older SLIP system is widely used in the USA, not so widely in the UK where PPP is often the norm. But if you do have a choice then the word is to use PPP, which is more up to date than SLIP and should be more reliable over modems. It's rumoured to be faster and less error-prone too, but as modems don't provide anything like an optimum link for data transfer this is difficult to quantify. There are concerns amongst technology nerds that PPP takes longer to negotiate its start-up link than SLIP but you're unlikely to notice this in practice. The author uses SLIP on a Mac and PPP on a Windows PC to the same provider with nary a problem, so the real answer must be – if it ain't broke don't swap it for something else that might be, because someone else says so.

You will almost always have to write a script within the SLIP or PPP handler to log you into the remote connection. Internet providers have much fun in changing the prompt at their end of the connection, so that all of the login scripts used by subscribers will suddenly fail to connect until changed. The amusement factor is compounded by the fact that if you cannot log in – you can't find that message telling you the login routine has been changed, and any Internet provider worth their salt will post messages about intended login changes days or weeks in advance.

Both SLIP and PPP utilities need to be configured with all sorts of information, like the phone number of the place you are going to connect to, and your Internet address (we're coming to that in a minute). What you should get from a decent supplier is a modicum of help in setting these things up, because in all truth, fighting with modems, SLIP and IP addresses will tax the brain of even the most enlightened comms guru. This includes the author, who admits to not having a beard, but also to not being a comms guru. This crafty person therefore got Demon Internet Services around on a pretence to fix up the dialling and address routines in exchange for a cup of tea. In fact most UK providers will offer at least a partial get-you-going service, with telephone help if you need it. You might also consider lugging your computer around to the Internet provider to have the software installed, just as you would take your Fiat Uno to the garage to have a radio installed. But phone the provider first, huh? You should expect to pay a fee for this service if it's offered, as it takes longer than you would expect.

Getting the right address

All this stuff about software is going to be of no use to you if you don't have an Internet address. An address is a place where you can normally be found, or at least where your mail will get sent to in the normal run of things. Everybody has an address – you can mail the Queen at Buck House, London, and the letter will get there. You can mail 'That Old Fool, Houses of Parliament, London', and the letter will go to the Prime Minister. For Internet mail, and everything else, you'll need an Internet address.

Internet addresses are peculiar things. They use numbers, because that's how things are with computers. And because there

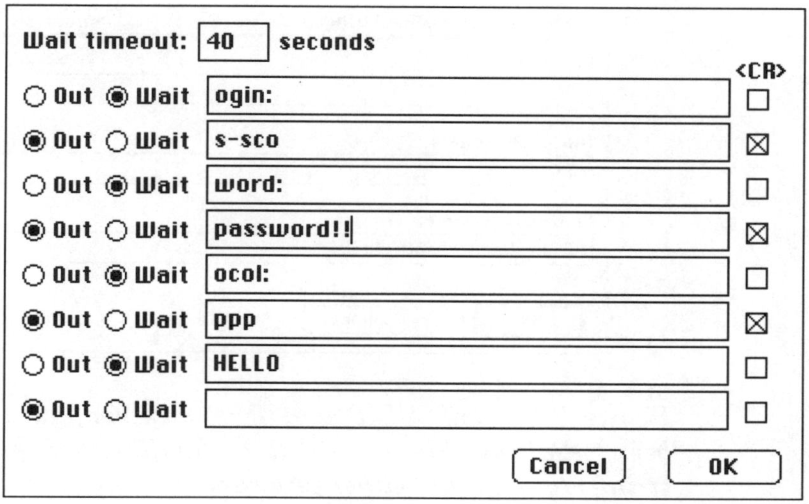

Figure 3.3 *PPP Login script. It's identical to a SLIP script, except for the line that tells the server to use PPP.*

are a lot of computers on the Internet you need a lot of numbers to describe them all. Numbers are allocated to providers on a block basis and become part of something called the Domain Name System (DNS). If you set up a TCP/IP network in your back bedroom and then hook it up to the Internet, you'll find all sorts of problems if the numbering scheme you've used clashes with the numbering scheme in the Big Wide World.

Why? Imagine that your long-lost Postal Order has arrived, and you go and buy 255 computers with the money. When you finally get out of the asylum you might want to hook them all together into one quite large network. So you'd give each one an address, perhaps starting at 1 and finishing at 255. This would be OK until your friend also got out of the asylum and wanted to hook his 255 computers up to yours. If his numbering system started at 256 then you'd have no problems – but naturally he's used the same numbering system as you have, and one of you will have to renumber a whole set of machines to give each one a unique address. It's the same with Internet addresses. No two can be the same, for obvious reasons, and so there's an entire body of people

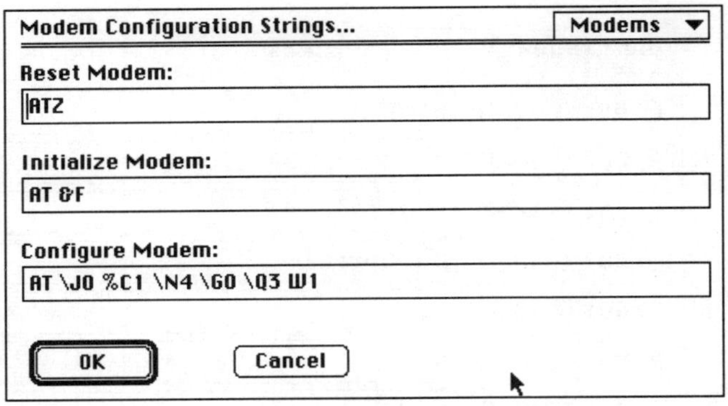

Figure 3.4 *Both SLIP and PPP will configure the modem before dialling. You'll need to be familar with modem set-up strings to configure either program.*

dishing out and managing Internet addressing. You as a punter won't need to worry, because your Internet provider has been allocated a block of addresses, and will let you use one if you pay your bills on time. You'll only have to worry if you've used a private numbering scheme on a non-Internet network, and you suddenly want to hook in. You'll have to change your addressing scheme to suit. Corporates take note!

Letters and figures

The Internet uses 32-bit binary numbers, that is, a series of 1s and 0s, to denote a single address. But because nobody understands binary, that string of digits is broken down into four 8-bit bytes, and then translated into a decimal number. So a decimal Internet address looks like 158.152.24.106, and the more eagle-eyed amongst you will spot that this string of numbers is the Internet address of the author. In fact, all this talk about Internet binary and decimal addresses is a bit spurious because you can use the Internet without stuffing your head full of numbers. Those decimal addresses are actually translated into textual address strings (in fact it happens the other way around) and 158.152.24.106 actually means S-SCO. DEMON.CO.UK. You can use either numbers or text addresses when sending mail or setting up your SLIP or PPP connection, as the text gets translated into the numeric address on the way. It's slightly faster to use the numerical form, although you're not going to notice this over a modem connection.

If you want to impress people in restaurants you can spout the Secret Lore of Internet Addressing. This states that you can tell a lot from a decimal Internet address and bore people to death with the result. In the example my address has a network number of 158.152. There will be loads of other people with 158.152 in their address, because that's the number of the network to which my computer is connected (over a modem or otherwise). My local address is 24.106 – which denotes the host computer on the 158.152 network itself. Networks are also subdivided into Class types but you don't need to know about these unless you're setting up or managing largish networks.

All this stuff about numbers is confusing, so let's forget it. From now on we should use letters, and dip a furtive toe into the Domain Name System. This is a convention which uses a three-letter suffix to the textual address. COM is used for a commercial company, EDU for an educational site, NET for networking sites, INT for international people like NATO, MIL for military (doesn't that include NATO?) and ORG for anything that doesn't fit any of the previous descriptions. There's also GOV for Governmental sites. DNS knows about national demarcations too, and assigns a country code; UK is the UK and CH is Switzerland, not the CHeck Republic, which is CZ – not CK, naturally. Other countries have their own codes.

If you decided to set up your own network, like our friend the loony, you could use LOONY.CO.UK for the domain, and then various machine names at that domain. Machine 1 could be called MARMITE.LOONY.CO.UK, and its user would then add a username: KEVIN@MARMITE.LOONY.CO.UK. Machine 2 could be called BOVRIL.LOONY.CO.UK and its user added as BRIAN@BOVRIL.LOONY.CO.UK. (Now doesn't that just tell you a lot about technology writers?) Oh, and UNIX people like to see addresses in lower case. This is because anything in upper case startles them, and they have to go and lie down in a dark room for a while. So you write address information in lower case as in ***kevin@marmite.loony.co.uk***.

Internet addresses are easy to understand and remember – once you decide to stick to alphabetical DNS descriptions instead of numbers. Want to practise? You might mail ***president@whitehouse.gov*** or even ***vice.president***

@whitehouse.gov and you'll receive a reply. This is because Americans know all about computers at birth, and some of their political leaders even have enough brains to be able to use them. Unfortunately mailing ***idiot@housecommons.gov*** won't get to the Prime Minister or anyone else, because UK Parliamentarians by and large haven't yet got the hang of this tricky computer stuff, although they might do once this book gets published. So if you want to help lever your country into the computer age, write immediately to your MP at the House of Commons, enclosing the ISBN of this book and a handsome letter of endorsement. And copy the same letter to at least 50 other names picked at random from the phone book. Every little helps.

Client–server jargon

There's more jargon in the wacky world of the Internet than in the whole of computerdom. We've already mentioned TCP/IP, domains and addresses, but you'll need to grasp the concept of client–server operations before you step out, blind and naked, onto the 'Net.

Client–server operation is simple. You the client (Wooster) say to the server (Jeeves), 'Go and get me a Martini, or those messages I haven't read, or that file I want'. The server will either have access to Martinis or messages or files, or it won't. If it doesn't you'll get a message saying so. If it does you'll get the result you want. Client–server operation tends to put the bulk of the processing for a computer-happening at the server end, leaving the client (local) end free for other things. In contrast, the file-server model simply lets computers connected to the file server grab files (and save them), which is what you get with a dial-up *terminal* connection. The Internet uses the client–server system, your local dial-up bulletin board probably uses the file-server system.

Finally...

Don't worry about learning any of the jargon in this chapter, until you decide you need it. You can get connected to the Internet without jargon, and indeed it should be the job of Internet providers to make this happen. At least you should know now:

- whether you want a terminal connection or a full network connection;
- that you need TCP/IP for a full connection, and SLIP or PPP (or a Windows Socket) if you want to use a modem;
- that you need a recognized Internet address to make everything work over TCP/IP links;
- that you don't need more jargon than this to get going.

Part 2

Internet tools

4 Electronic mail (email)

'As yet you can't contact the Prime Minister by email...'

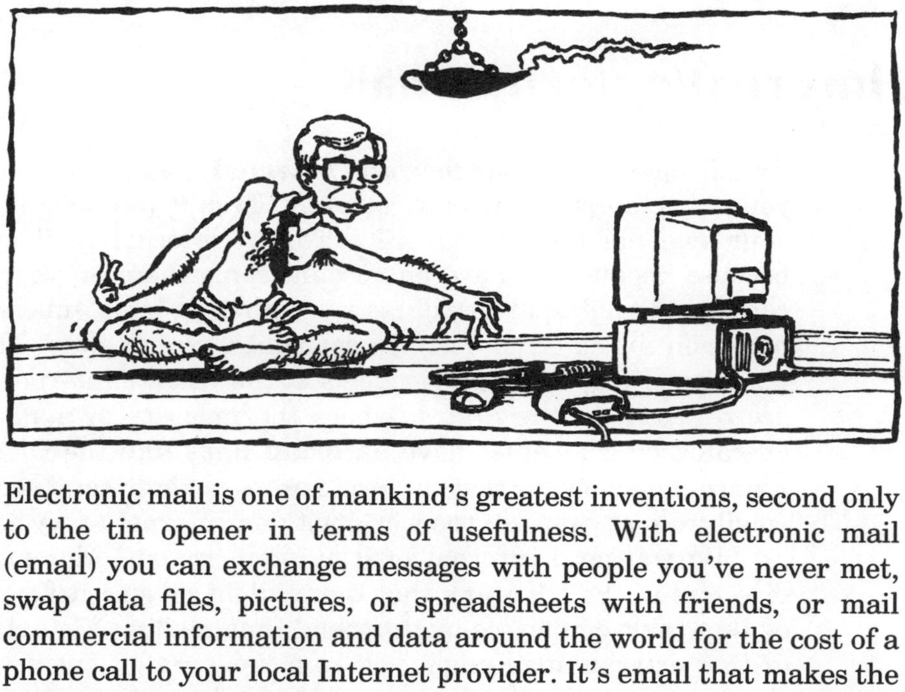

Electronic mail is one of mankind's greatest inventions, second only to the tin opener in terms of usefulness. With electronic mail (email) you can exchange messages with people you've never met, swap data files, pictures, or spreadsheets with friends, or mail commercial information and data around the world for the cost of a phone call to your local Internet provider. It's email that makes the world go round, and it's email at which the Internet is particularly good.

Email has several advantages over other forms of electronic communication. It's better than fax (for straight text) because it's cheaper, and you don't need to chop down trees to receive a message. It's also more flexible – it's much cheaper to electronically 'cc' a message to ten people than to fax to ten different numbers, because you don't need to send ten messages. One message goes to your email service, and the mail handler there distributes it. And email is automatic – if a message comes into your mailbox you can generally access it from any telephone in the world, whereas a paper fax needs to be manually redirected. And email gets past those bad-tempered secretaries who 'edit' faxes to their boss. Email the Head of British Telecom and he will get the message, not some top-heavy bint brought in to decorate the place for a day.

From a corporate point of view email saves money, and Bill Gates, the richest PC owner in the world, says, 'I couldn't run my business without email'. So if you want to communicate with 20 million Internet users, 2 million CompuServe users, and Bill Gates – get yourself a computer equipped with a modem, and an Internet email address.

Internal/external mail

Email comes in various flavours. **Internal** mail is what you get if you set up a system in your company. Even if you have links with your regional offices you still have an internal mail system – because people who have an account somewhere on your system can't send mail to external users on other systems, unless there's provision for external users to get mail via a gateway. The great majority of corporate mail systems in the UK are internal. Things are different in the States, where the majority of mail systems operated by companies have **external** links into the wide world. External mail means that corporate users can both send and receive email from any user in the world with an Internet-savvy account.

Do you need external mail on your system? Many company directors in the UK think that there might be a security problem, or that their employees might spend time mailing Virtual Valerie, or that external mail might just be a time-waster, but if you're in the business of selling any sort of product then you need an Internet-savvy mail system. If you don't have one, the competition, especially in the States, certainly has.

Email brings huge benefits to individual users too. This book, for instance, couldn't have been written without it. Quite often it was common for the book, or matters relating directly to it, to generate ten or more messages a day. Email brings communication, and communication generally brings benefits, and Internet email is so far the most cost-efficient method of long-distance text communication yet invented.

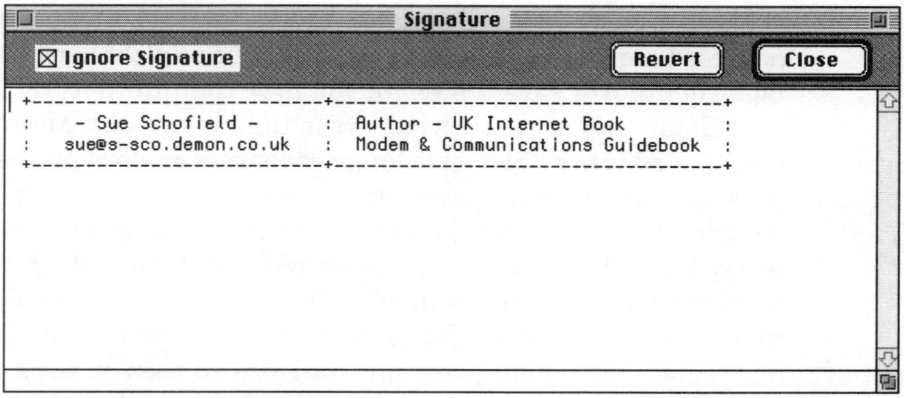

Figure 4.1 *Automatic signature generation in VersaTerm.*

All about email

Email works in the same way as ordinary postal mail, except the carrier is the Internet, not the Royal Mail. You construct a message by putting the address of the recipient at the top, followed by the main text. Your email program takes care of adding your own address, and a heap of other things too, like adding your signature automatically to the bottom of files, sorting out binary (data) files from plain text, and so on. Email programs vary in their capabilities from platform to platform, but their basic function is to make the construction, sending and receiving of email as painless as possible.

If your computer is already hooked up to the Internet, or you have a dial-up terminal or network connection, then the chances are you are the possessor of an Internet-savvy mail address. It's important to know whether this is the case or not, because if you don't have an Internet mail address then you can't receive mail from external Internet users. Many of the bulletin board systems in the UK have cottoned onto the fact that they can make money by selling email addresses and most of the larger systems now offer you this facility. Even smaller services are catching up. It's likely that most of the commercial dial-up services of any size will eventually provide Internet email and if you are thinking of signing up with a dial-up service provider, large or small, then you shouldn't part with real money unless you get an Internet mail address thrown in. Otherwise you'll feel a complete nerd when your boss/client/lover says 'I'll email you over the Internet'.

Email programs are a subject in their own right. Many of them will append binary files such as spreadsheets or word processor data to your mail as enclosures, not a few of them provide basic or complex text encryption, and some of the really good ones actually work. Your choice of mail program will depend on which computer platform you are using, and what level of service is provided at the server (remote) end of things, but by and large you shouldn't pay out money for a mail program until you've seen it work with the service you're going to be using. If you are still using DOS or a similar line editor to read and write your mail messages then you're missing out a little – because there are some good mail programs around for Windows users. The cost of email programs isn't really an issue, because there is a lot of free and nearly free email software around for all platforms.

Tricky bits – the mechanics of email

How email gets to and from your machine is a source of wonder and frustration. You'd think that something like a straightforward ASCII message would be easy to ship around a network, but like all things to do with computers, and especially to do with UNIX, email seems to be a particularly complex subject to master. But the basics are, well, basic.

Remember all that stuff about domains earlier on? Email addresses contain domain information, plus a little bit about the user. At its most basic, the first part of a mail address is the username. The second part (after the @ symbol) is the descriptor of the machine that's handling the collation and storage of your incoming mail. After the address comes the body text of the message, and the last bit is the signature. Dial-up users have their mail stored by their service provider, who then sends it to them when they log in. If you have a direct Internet connection you generally don't have to do anything to get your mail, other than

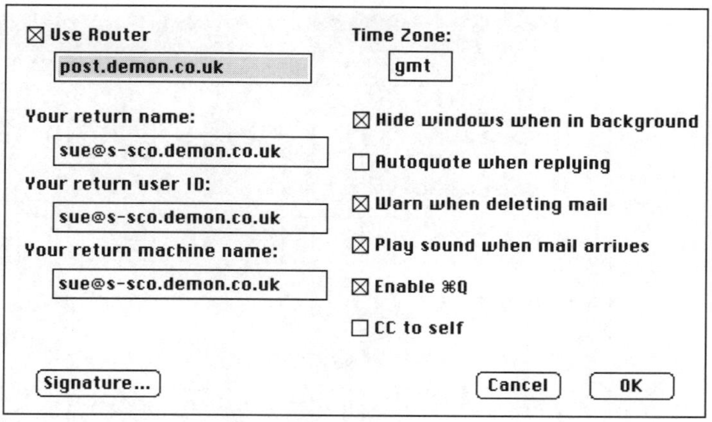

Figure 4.2 *Setting up mail gateways in Leemail, a Mac mail program.*

start your local mail handling program and perhaps type in a password.

There are different ways in which mail is handled at remote servers, and differences in methods of getting mail to the recipient, but the essentials are straightforward. Look at the email system as being an infinitely long river into which people can chuck parcels. The river eventually goes over a weir upon which stands your butler armed with a long stick. You've told your butler that every time he sees a parcel with your name on it he is to fish it out of the river and give it to you when you next turn up for lunch. If you're not in, Jeeves will put the mail in a mailbox so that you can pop in and collect it at your convenience.

In this analogy your butler is working as a mail handler. So if you want to send mail to the author via this method you would address it to sue@s-sco.demon.co.uk, but it would actually be held by a server called post.demon.co.uk. It's the mail handling server which looks at all incoming mail to demon.co.uk, slices out mail addressed to its users and forwards mail on when users log in. In fact all you have to remember is that, for modem users, your mail has to be stored somewhere on a server, so that it's there the next time you log in.

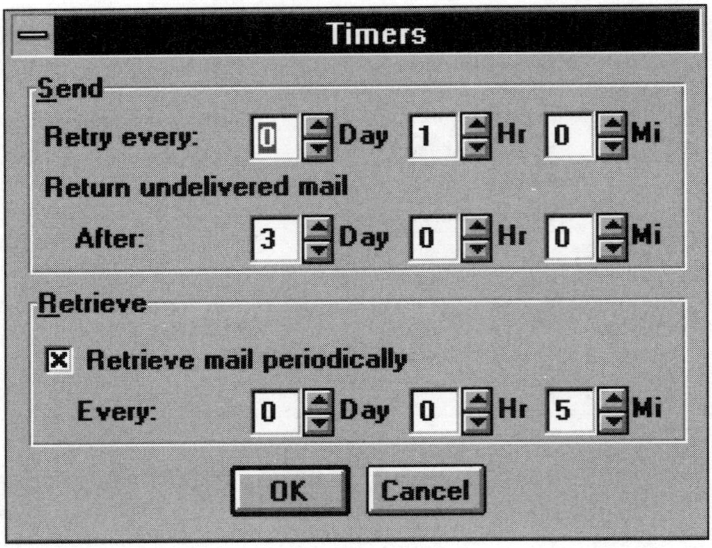

Figure 4.3 *The smart mail timer feature in Internet Chameleon.*

The politics of mail provision

Some UK Internetters will often be presented with a choice when they ask their service providers about mail provision. Your service provider will offer something called SMTP mail or POP mail, occasionally both, and sometimes something called UUCP.

SMTP is the Simple Mail Transfer Protocol, so called because it isn't. The other common offering is POP mail, currently in a third reincarnation and called POP3 mail. UUCP is UNIX to UNIX Copy Program – which on the face of it doesn't look much like the name of a proper mail program. It still doesn't look like a proper mail program when you get close up to it, and UUCP mail is best avoided, unless you have no real alternative. You won't find much UUCP stuff unless you work in a UNIX house, and even then you'll notice that most people have found something better. UUCP mail addresses are different to most other forms of email addressing, and if you see something with exclamation marks dividing up the address then it's UUCP.

But back to SMTP, which works by loitering with intent

outside your mailbox back at the service provider's office. When mail comes in SMTP tries to forward it to the destination machine. If that machine isn't available SMTP will keep trying for about three days. If it still can't deliver after that time SMTP will often give up. Moral: make a habit of getting your mail daily.

The other common mail handling system is POP3 (which stands for Post Office Protocol, third attempt) and is a deal more complex. You run a POP3 client on your machine, and tell it to go and get the mail, rather than wait for it to be sent. POP3 is also a bit more flexible than SMTP – you can tell the POP3 server to deliver your mail to another address, which might come in handy if you are going to work in a different office – and it has the advantage of being supported by a large number of email programs.

One important thing to watch out for is that some of the Shareware mail client programs (the ones that run on your personal computer) will use SMTP to send mail and POP3 to receive it. If your service provider only provides SMTP and the mail program you have needs POP3, you'll have to use two programs to handle your mail – one to send stuff out, one to retrieve it. Provision of SMTP mail only is less common than it once was, especially as Windows and Mac users tend to prefer POP3 mail because most of the Shareware email programs for those two platforms support it. However, there's a catch with the implementation of POP3 from some suppliers such as Demon. In the case of Demon, if you have their POP3 mail server sending your mail, you won't be able to have multiple mail addresses at your sub-domain – or rather, all mail for any user at your domain will be sent to anyone who logs in to the domain with POP3 software and the password for the POP3 server. In the USA most users won't worry about having two or more users at the same account for the same fee – they simply open a second account.

On the other hand, most UK users will not have access to POP3 mail from that supplier – which means they'll need to use a commercial SMTP program such as NetManage Chameleon for Windows – or if they're Mac users, they'll need either AddMail and Eudora, or LeeMail and Eudora to both send and receive mail. They will not be able to use otherwise widespread mail programs such as PC Eudora because of the lack of POP3 provision. (Chameleon can handle both SMTP and POP3 mail.)

This SMTP send and POP3 receive issue is going to be a big

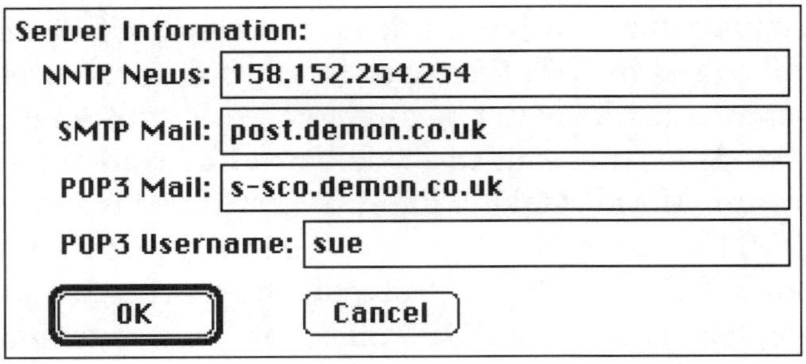

Figure 4.4 *Setting SMTP and POP3 mail options.*

one in 1995 because, regardless of what some UK suppliers decide to implement, the largest provision of email software is going to come from the USA. Already there are new commercial versions of the fine Eudora program for Macs and Windows machines, and as we've seen, standard programs such as Eudora need a 'standard' combination of SMTP and POP3 mail to work at all.

If you are opening an account for your Windows machine and your Internet provider doesn't provide a choice of POP3 or SMTP (or both) – ask them what the alternative options are. If you're stuck with SMTP only mail and you want to use Windows or Mac Shareware mail programs you'll have to use two or more of those programs to get the most from your email. This is a ludicrous proposition when computers are supposed to be getting easier to use. As an example, the finest all round integrated Mail/Usenet/FTP and telnet program for any platform is VersaTerm Link for the Mac, yet it can't be used with the standard Demon Internet service (at the time of writing) because of their lack of POP3 provision. Demon's POP3 service will cost you £180.00 net per year extra, if you decide that you want to use Eudora software with your machine. Other suppliers take note.

If you are using a terminal Internet connection such as any of the many BBS based mail hook-ups, then you can dismiss all this stuff about POP3 and SMTP. Your service provider will simply put all your mail into your standard mailbox. You'll get it when you log in and ask for it. In some ways this is an ideal situation if you just want quick and easy access to your mail, and in fact the majority of UK journalists still use this method for sending electronic text around. The disadvantage is that a terminal connection cannot generally provide you with direct hooks into the Internet, and binary files sent this way will need a separate decoder routine. You won't be able to use a mail program with a built-in UUdecode or BinHex ASCII descrambler in fully automatic mode to turn those messages back into spreadsheets or files.

Mail program facilities

So what do you look out for when buying, borrowing or stealing a mail program for Internet use? You'll need basic text editing features, such as backspace, delete, plus cursor movements, and cut & paste will also be invaluable. Spelling checkers are useful, but if you are going to mail a message of more than a few lines, presumably you'll create it in a word processor and then paste it into a mail program. An address book is vital, as is the ability to copy mail (cc) to more than one person. Group addressing is also handy for corporates, or mail freaks who have to tell everyone about everything. Group addressing lets you create a set of addressees with a single title, in the address book, and the entire set of addressees will get the message if it's sent to the group as a whole. But one of the most useful facilities is a reply generator. You click a button marked 'reply' – and the software creates the reply message header and dumps part or the whole of the message to which you are replying into the text editor, preceded by > marks. You then dive in and edit the pertinent bits of what the sender said, appending your own replies. Sounds complex? Look at this:

> and furthermore you'll be hearing from my solicitors anon (line from original message preceded by >)

I've never heard of a solicitor called anon. Is this a joke? (reply text)

sue

Both lines of text get sent back in the message, and the signature is added automatically.

Things to do with email

You've got the account set up, mastered the software and even maybe thought that personal computers can actually be used for something useful. So what do you do with your new email service? Well, you can mail the author for a start, as at least that way you'll be able to tell if your mail is working. You'll get a reply of sorts as the author has a stock of ill-mannered mail messages she keeps for replying to people who buy her books. Then you can practise your Smiley skills. Smileys, or 'emoticons' as the Americans like to call them, are ASCII characters used to make a picture. 'Picture' in this context is stretching things a bit, but a colon, a hyphen, and a close-bracket sign placed together thus :-) and viewed sideways make a Smiley face. Other nonsensical trivia abound. There are sad faces, faces with glasses, pictures of the Pope, pictures of the Pope with glasses on, pictures of the Pope on the loo, and more. All you have to do is to look at them from the right angle. Of course, if you're a wizard wordsmith you won't ever need to use a Smiley, because people will know from your lucid text whether you are being humorous, or just your normal obnoxious self. You might even send your boss an email which says 'You're a snivelling exploitative git' and put a Smiley after it to show you're only joking. You're sure to be excused and given a pay rise for being so inventive.

The author actually hates emoticons because they are slowly replacing the English language in the real world and even the national newspapers have started to use them. That way they don't have to pay for proper writers. But when you're young, or a newcomer to the Internet, or 'write' for a newspaper, being obnoxious hardly matters. :-)

By the way, the Internet contains heaps of other ASCII images. The Usenet group ***alt.ascii.art*** is full of pictures laboriously created out of ASCII characters in much the same way one might create a model of the Eiffel Tower out of matchsticks. It's art, Jim, but not as we know it.

Things to do with email, Part II

This section is for those readers who didn't believe me and have signed up with a terminal service provider such as CIX,

CompuServe, or any one of the burgeoning numbers of UK based bulletin boards attached to the Internet by way of their Internet-savvy mail addressing.

In English that means that you can do an awful lot with just an email account – without access to FTP or Archie or any other of those complicated bits of TCP/IP based software. You can do an awful lot more *with* them, but that info is in the following chapters.

There are a couple of caveats; most terminal accounts charge by the minute or second for your time on line, and not a few charge per Internet message received, or the amount of storage space taken up by your incoming mail. As always, check the small print carefully before you go requesting megabytes of data to be sent to your mail account – it could cost you a lot of money.

Here's a small summary of what's available to you if you only have an email account. It may be more than enough for many readers:

- *Archie file searches*: Want to know where to find recipes for Mississippi Mud Pie or that file containing the Windows screen saver with Santa on it? Archie can interact with emailers – see Chapter 7.

- *Mail-lists*: Your email software becomes a library of incoming information – everything from Aardvarks to Xenophobes is covered in the LISTSERV system. See this chapter and Chapter 5 for more info.

- *Electronic magazines (Zines)*: These are often available by email direct from the compiler. LISTSERV has most of the details, the new batch of UK Internet magazines will carry the rest.

- *Electronic shopping*: A number of suppliers now sell mail order by electronic mail. Details are now published on the World Wide Web, along with pictures of the products – the email addresses of suppliers can often be found in the technology pages of the national papers.

- *Electronic file transfer*: You can get files from Internet sites equipped with FTPMAIL which does what you'd imagine – it sends you files by mail. It's a bit like fishing by remote control from the moon, but briefly you send mail to a FTPMAIL server, ask for an index, and then use that to select the files you want. Before you get hot under the collar with the thought of having all those files mailed to you for free, remember that you may be paying a charge to your service provider for downloading the subsequent huge mail message, the FTP directory command system you'll have to battle with will be in UNIX, and you'll have to use UUdecode or BinHeX to turn the file into an executable. And each time you want a list of a directory you'll have to send a new message. FTPMAIL is time consuming. If these difficulties only add spice to your Internet pudding then full details of FTPMAIL are in Chapter 8. Start saving for the subsequent phone and divorce bills now.

There's a lot more for email users but you should at least get a flavour of what you can do with email from the above. In most cases email is by far the most important aspect of Internet use for many people, and if you are prepared to lose out a little on TCP/IP access then a terminal account with an Internet-savvy email address is the next best thing.

In the UK many corporate email accounts are now Internet savvy – that is, they can send and receive from other Internet addresses and if that's the case with your email account at work then you should have access to all of the above. Some corporates limit access to incoming mail but this is rare. Send a message to the Author at sue@s-sco.demon.co.uk if you want to try out your external mail. If you don't get a reply the chances are that she's emigrated with the winner of the National Lottery, or more likely, your corporate mail system doesn't permit external mail.

Mail-lists

Email lists are slightly further up the ladder of human endeavour. A mail-list is something you join, and in the course of a few hours or days, you receive endless messages covering the sphere of interest you enquired about. Mail-lists seem like quite a Good Idea when you're a techno-tyro, but their novelty wears off the day your first phone bill arrives. Some of the mail-lists are quite informative. You can have the White House mail you with the President's agenda for the day and then wonder just what the heck he does on his days off, which seem to occur about once every three days. Other lists cover national or regional issues, or aspects of human

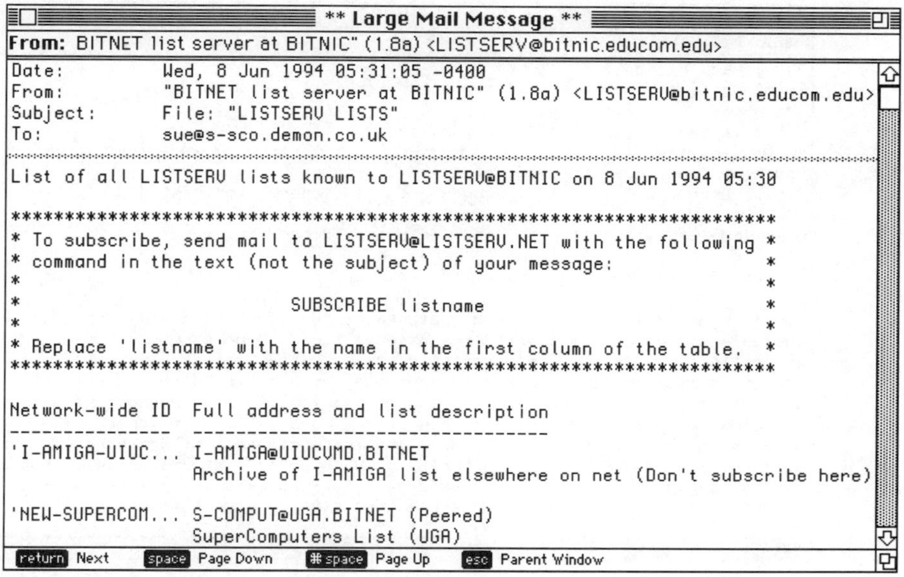

```
** Large Mail Message **
From: BITNET list server at BITNIC" (1.8a) <LISTSERV@bitnic.educom.edu>
Date:        Wed, 8 Jun 1994 05:31:05 -0400
From:        "BITNET list server at BITNIC" (1.8a) <LISTSERV@bitnic.educom.edu>
Subject:     File: "LISTSERV LISTS"
To:          sue@s-sco.demon.co.uk

List of all LISTSERV lists known to LISTSERV@BITNIC on 8 Jun 1994 05:30

*******************************************************************
* To subscribe, send mail to LISTSERV@LISTSERV.NET with the following *
* command in the text (not the subject) of your message:              *
*                                                                     *
*                      SUBSCRIBE listname                             *
*                                                                     *
* Replace 'listname' with the name in the first column of the table.  *
*******************************************************************

Network-wide ID  Full address and list description
---------------  --------------------------------
'I-AMIGA-UIUC... I-AMIGA@UIUCVMD.BITNET
                 Archive of I-AMIGA list elsewhere on net (Don't subscribe here)

'NEW-SUPERCOM... S-COMPUT@UGA.BITNET (Peered)
                 SuperComputers List (UGA)
return Next   space Page Down   ⌘space Page Up   esc Parent Window
```

Figure 4.5 *Listservs can generate large amounts of incoming mail. This is a list of mailing lists...*

sexuality, or what to do with that model of the Eiffel Tower you made out of matchsticks.

Mail-lists vary in content and interest. Many mail-lists contain stuff other people have mailed in. You post a message to the list server, and everyone else on the list gets a copy, whether they like it or not. They are called *reflector* lists. Other mail-lists are assembled by the list owner, who then sends out single-topic mail. Mail-List Digests are simply large files containing all the stuff mailed to the server by members. You get a huge mail-message or file containing hundreds of messages at a time. In both cases mail-lists can be moderated, that is, have offensive or off-topic stuff edited out by the list moderator. While moderating mail (and Usenet groups) might seem like censorship, many aspects of Internet mail and messaging benefit from a small amount of control. On the other hand, too much control makes the moderator seem like a totalitarian ogre to his victims, and there's often a very fine line between the two extremes.

Mail-lists can be fun, especially if you can find one which hits your particular interest spot on, but it's often harder to get off one

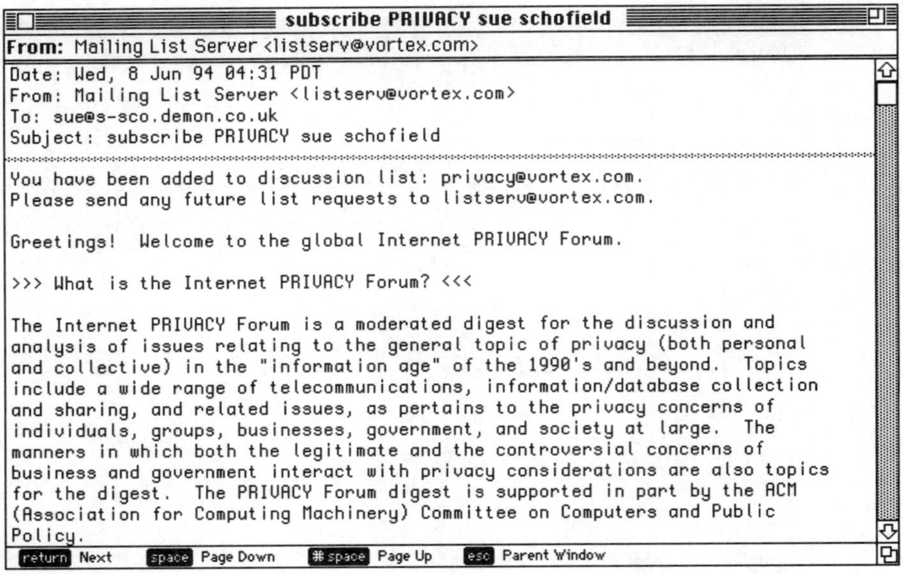
subscribe PRIVACY sue schofield

From: Mailing List Server <listserv@vortex.com>

Date: Wed, 8 Jun 94 04:31 PDT
From: Mailing List Server <listserv@vortex.com>
To: sue@s-sco.demon.co.uk
Subject: subscribe PRIVACY sue schofield

You have been added to discussion list: privacy@vortex.com.
Please send any future list requests to listserv@vortex.com.

Greetings! Welcome to the global Internet PRIVACY Forum.

>>> What is the Internet PRIVACY Forum? <<<

The Internet PRIVACY Forum is a moderated digest for the discussion and analysis of issues relating to the general topic of privacy (both personal and collective) in the "information age" of the 1990's and beyond. Topics include a wide range of telecommunications, information/database collection and sharing, and related issues, as pertains to the privacy concerns of individuals, groups, businesses, government, and society at large. The manners in which both the legitimate and the controversial concerns of business and government interact with privacy considerations are also topics for the digest. The PRIVACY Forum digest is supported in part by the ACM (Association for Computing Machinery) Committee on Computers and Public Policy.

return Next space Page Down ⌘space Page Up esc Parent Window

Figure 4.6 *Mail from the Privacy Listserv.*

than to get on. To sign on to many lists you simply send a mail message saying 'Subscribe me' or some such, and you'll be on the list. To leave, you send a message saying 'Resign' or 'Unsubscribe' or similar. Often it gets ignored. Many mail-lists now have 'intelligent' software that lets you pick and choose which topics you want to receive from the lists, and in what order or format, and the White House system is a good example.

Nerds, geeks and mail-bombing

The Internet being what it is, someday you are going to upset someone. You'll post an inoffensive message in a Usenet group, and sure as eggs is eggs you'll get mail back, public or otherwise, casting aspersions upon your parentage. In truth there's not much in the way of offensive private mail most of the time, and you're unlikely to be waylaid by other Internet users, but if you do post something contentious you are going to upset someone. And if it's a really badly placed message you'll be mail-bombed – a scenario where revengeful Internet geeks mail you with huge files which clog up

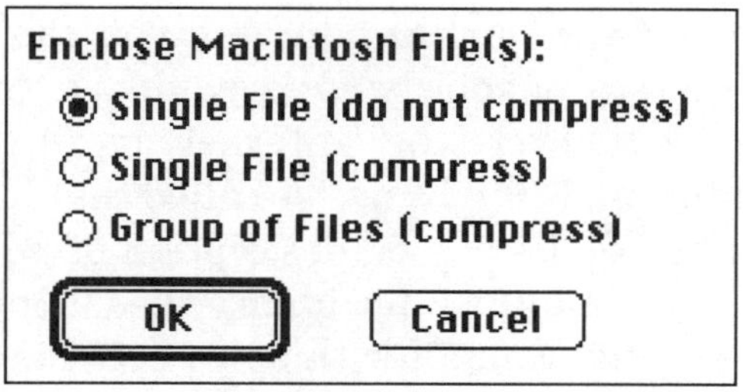

Figure 4.7 *Mailing files with email. Decent mail programs let you attach files to the message. Binary files are automatically encoded into ASCII, with a button marked Enclosures, or File Attachments.*

your mailbox. This doesn't happen a lot, but there have been some cases where particularly offensive (or famous) people have been mail-bombed. In any case it makes sense to set a limit on the size of mail messages you can receive, especially if you're using a list server to mail you. The NATO list server is particularly fond of mailing out messages of 30–40 kilobytes, which can be expensive to download over a modem. Most decent mail programs have a facility to let you set the size limit. Some have options which change long email messages into files, which are then copied to your hard disk as text files. This works well for binary files sent to you as email (mail attachments).

If you are getting obscene or threatening mail then your first port of call is your Internet provider to ask for this mail to be intercepted. But be aware that many of the terminals and workstations connected to the Internet in universities can be operated anonymously, and often there's little chance of tracking down the origins of *ad hoc* obscene or threatening mail.

Mail attachments

A mail attachment is something you attach to an email message. It takes the form of a binary file which is embedded into the text of the message (usually just below the main body of text) and it's a great way of sending real data around the world. A binary file can be a spreadsheet file, a graphic file or digitized photograph, or a complete software application, and you can send binary files over the Internet to anyone who is equipped to collect them. Binary files are sent over the Internet by a process called ASCII Representation. It might not be called that in any other book on the Internet, but that's a good description of how it works. In fact the Internet can't handle 8-bit binary files as produced by these new-fangled personal computer thingies because it's a 7-bit system and personal computers use 8 bits. So binary 8-bit data files are encoded into a 7-bit representation of their hexadecimal codes, and then fired over the Internet as email. At the receiving end the ASCII text is decoded back into binary, and the result is a reconstruction of the original file.

The actual program tool you need to achieve this small miracle varies depending on which computer and which mail software you are using. PC and Amiga owners can use variants of UUencode and UUdecode, whilst Mac users need BinHex, a single utility which provides both coding and decoding functions. However, most of the better commercial mail programs will handle code/decode functions automatically for you, and at both ends too. All you have to do is set up a document with the address of the recipient in it, add a few lines of text to say what's happening, and click on the 'attachment' or 'enclosure' button. The program then picks up the data file and does the rest. Alas, in the world of DOS, where things just haven't caught up with clicky-button technology, attaching a file can mean an awkward process of encoding the file and sending it with two different programs. But Mac and Windows users will find all of the hard work done for them – if they get a half-decent mail program.

Once you get the hang of the need for converting files for transfer you can use this method for transferring data files from DOS to Macs, and vice versa. You might, for instance, want to transfer Word for Mac files into Word for Windows. You just code them into ASCII, ship them over the net as email, and your Windows-owning colleague on the other side of the world can load them straight into his PC.

There are some emergent 'standards' for attaching binary files to mail. One of them is MIME – Multipurpose Internet Mail Extension – and there are others fighting for dominance. MIME is perhaps the one you'll hear most about, as the business community are now paying lots of money for MIME-compliant email systems.

Internet-hostile mail systems

Once word gets around that you have an Internet account you'll probably be asked to send binary mail files to people. While you can certainly send ordinary ASCII text to anyone else in the world who has an Internet-savvy mail address, life gets complicated when you need to send or receive binary files. Things are more complicated than they should be in the UK especially, mainly because there are thousands of bulletin board systems in this country which sprang into being before Internet usage became widespread. In the UK the subculture of modem and electronic communication users revolves, not around the Internet as it does in the States, but around large dial-up systems such as CIX and CompuServe. Both of these systems use mutually exclusive methods to transfer files between subscribers, and you cannot (at the time of writing) use your newly found Internet mail skills to directly send a binary file to either of these two systems – except as a binary-coded ASCII mail message. CompuServe looks like being the first to break the deadlock and is revising its Internet interface to provide a more usable front-end for users. This might, or might not, provide an easy way for Internet users to send files to CompuServe users. At the very least CompuServe could release a new version of their Mac and Windows based front-end systems (called MacCim and WinCim respectively), which will automatically handle the transfer of ASCII-encoded binary files. However, CompuServe users pay an extra fee for using Internet mail, so this option isn't likely to gather much support if it ever comes about.

There's a problem too for CIX users. CIX uses an internal method for binary file transfer called BINMAIL. BINMAIL doesn't work outside CIX, so you need a CIX account to be able to use it. If you need to transfer binary files to a CIX user you can only UUencode them and send them as mail.

Luckily, many corporates can send binary mail to CompuServe via a variety of electronic mail hubs, and if your company uses external electronic mail there's every chance that you can get binary files routed to CompuServe in this manner. You won't be able to do this with CIX and the hundreds of other UK-centric dial-up systems which use their own internal mail 'standards', so you'll have to use UUencode or its equivalent.

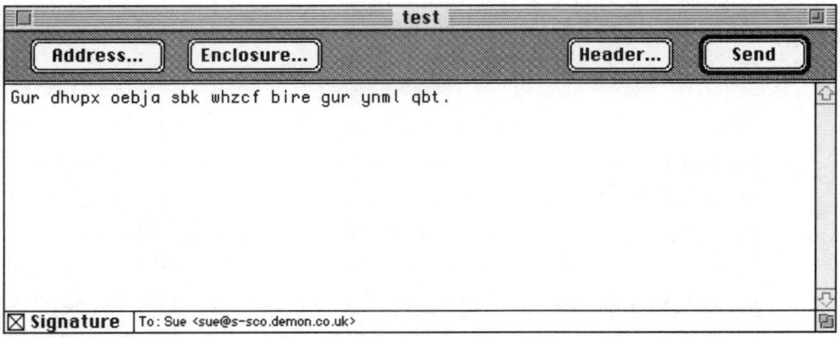

Figure 4.8 *A ROT13 message. The text says: The quick brown fox jumps over the lazy dog.*

Anonymous mail

If you are an observer of how complicated human beings are capable of making their, and other people's lives, one day you'll come across the phenomenon of anonymous mail. Unlike anonymous FTP, where the remote service pretends that it doesn't know or care who you are, (despite the fact it can read your domain address in each packet) anonymous mail is altogether more sinister.

Anonymous mail servers take a message from anyone, strip out all addressing information from the originating message, and then forward the rest of the message on to its destination. If the recipient has a sufficient lack of wit to reply, the anonymous server will pick up the reply, check the originator's address in a look-up table and mail the reply to him/her. Anonymous mail thus serves to bolster the poor image that the Internet has, and appears to be mainly used for sending abuse to Usenet Groups and celebrities.

It's real use, (if anything on the Internet was ever going to serve mankind with a useful purpose) is for contact with assistance groups such as AIDS and other help organizations. But anonymous mail often serves no real purpose, except to waste the lives of people who have it inflicted upon them.

Anonymous mail also comes from 'open' terminals in many US campuses, and the upcoming 'cybercafes' – where you pay real money for a virtual good time. Campus based open terminals often

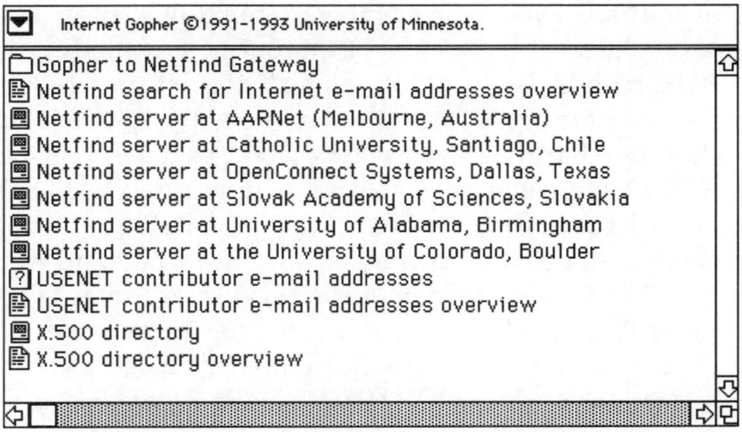

Figure 4.9 *Finding email addresses with Gopher.*

have a generic address, which will indicate the originating site in the message, but not the name of the originator who will use a nom-de-junk. Some campus based open terminals now automatically add a disclaimer to these messages, which in effect says that the obscene message you just got is being paid for by the US taxpayer as part of some mother's son's educational process.

Many Internet providers will automatically filter out messages from anonymous mail servers, and many commercial mail products have a feature which can be set up to reject mail from these sites. But if anonymous mail blights your phone bill then send the message, together with a reasonable and calm request to the Postmaster at the anonymous mail server concerned. Many of these are real people, and would not like to see full details of abuse of their service splashed across US or UK national papers, especially if they are inhabiting a site paid for by tax dollars, or pounds sterling.

Encrypt/decrypt

Mail over the Internet isn't as private as you might think. There have been numerous instances of mail being intercepted, and there are endless rumours that the FBI, the Inland Revenue, the CIA, and Jeremy Beadle all have secret hooks into private mail. To get over these fears many mail programs now provide encryption of text. The most basic encryption routine is something called ROT13. ROT stands for Rotation, and all the letters of the alphabet are rotated thirteen places forward in a ROT13 message. ROT13 is therefore hardly an encryption at all, as a five-year-old can decrypt ROT13 messages in a matter of minutes. So ROT13 is used to protect the endings of jokes in public mailings, or to keep sexually explicit material from the eyes of those who don't want to read it.

There are other more serious encryption schemes around. VersaTerm Link for the Mac provides a good one – but publishes the key as an appendix in the manual. At least it would baffle *ad hoc* lurkers for a while. PGP (Pretty Good Privacy) is another, as is the proposed Clipper system. But do you really need to encrypt your mail messages? The first thing to realize is that few people use encryption so you have to make sure that the recipient uses the same scheme. At the moment this is difficult if you use an Amiga and the recipient uses a BBC Micro or a NeXT Workstation.

If you do have commercially sensitive information to send over the Internet then you should look at some method of password-protecting it, at least. One easy way is to password-protect word processor or spreadsheet files in the application program, or to bundle files through a compressor program such as PKZip for the PC, Stuffit for the Mac, or LHA for the Amiga. These programs will produce a collection of files (called an archive) which can be password-protected and sent over the 'Net after being converted to ASCII in the normal way. Similarly you shouldn't mail your credit card details around, nor post messages which say 'I live at such and such address and my hobby is collecting rare diamonds' (or Macintosh computers) otherwise you'll be receiving mail from burglars asking you when you're going on your holidays. Unfortunately, they don't always ask.

The subject of mailing credit card numbers around is a thorny one. As the Internet continues to lean more towards Mammon than Academia there will be more commercial transactions carried out. At the moment many of the transactions between vendors and customers will require a credit card number, and generally speaking the Internet is not a safe place to leave credit card details suspended in Cyberspace. Many commercial vendors will dispute this (they would, wouldn't they), but there are an increasing number of programs around called Packet Sniffers. The sole purpose of these is to track IP packets travelling over a network, and log their contents to disk. Packet Sniffers generate huge amounts of logged data, and it takes a while to write algorithms to sort that data into human-readable form, but it can be done, and the format of credit card data is easy to distinguish from plain text traffic. So the answer is – at least be wary when mailing your credit card number around. There is a slim chance that it might be intercepted and misused, as happened to one William Gibson. Gibson is a cult Cyberspace guru and fiction scribbler, who found his credit card details being hunted down and then published on the 'Net by self-styled Cyberpunks. But then if you write a cult book called *Neuromancer*, what do you expect?

Finally, if you're female, you are going to have to face up to the fact that the Internet is a male-dominated phenomenon, and that it's used for everything from adolescent tribal posing to the distribution of material you wouldn't want your dog to see. General rule number one is that there are no general rules, general rule number two is not to give out your private address or phone number without good reason. There are documented cases of hairy psychopaths getting hold of email addresses and then selling subscriptions for Internet newsletters to the unfortunate recipients.

Sending mail to other addresses

It's all very well having all of this mail stuff at your fingertips, but there's a snag. How do you know who to send mail to? It would help if everyone who bought a modem was given an email address and had it tattooed on their forehead, but until this notion gets passed at the next Conservative Party conference we'll have to find another method. If you have an email address then at least publish it on your business card or letterhead, and stick it on the Christmas cards this year. It all helps make the electronic world go round.

If you want to send mail to other people you'll sometimes come across an address which makes little sense to you, or to the mail handling facilities you're using. Unfortunately there are few conventions for mail addressing outside the Internet, despite protestations from UNIX geeks that it's all perfectly straightforward. Want to send mail to user number 100113,2132 at CompuServe? You'll need to address it to 100113.2132@compuserve.com. Note that the comma in the address has been changed to a full stop, and the suffix 'com' has been added. Other mail services, such as those operated by IBM, are equally quirky, and the easiest way to get over this is to ask for an Internet-compliant mail address from your intended addressee. There are numerous lists of addressing conventions on commercial systems, and one notable one is published by Scott Yanoff on the 'Net. You can't read it here because Scott wanted 500 dollars cash before giving permission to publish on paper, despite his own protestations that the 'Net shouldn't be misused for profit motives. Funny old world, the Internet.

Bounced mail

Sending mail to addresses other than those on your own system is pretty much of an *ad hoc* affair, although most of the mail gets through most of the time. But it can take anything up to two days for mail to arrive, although the vast majority is delivered worldwide in a few hours. The biggest problems are caused by faulty addresses, and much mail is bounced (returned to sender if possible) because of this.

Bounced mail will be returned to you with a message in the header telling you why. Reasons vary from 'Host Unknown', where routing services can't find the part of the address after the @ sign, to 'User Unknown', where routing finds the bit of the address after the @ sign but can't find the user there. 'Service Unavailable' occurs where both user and host are found but the host computer there is not accepting mail because someone spilt Old El Paso Extra Hot Taco sauce into the hard disk. And 'Can't Send' happens because of network, or 'administrative' problems, where the recipient hasn't been paying his or her Internet provider's bills.

Fingering the pie

There are no real user-directory services on the Internet, so if some smart Alec in a shiny suit offers to sell you one, turn him away with a smile. Besides, any such directory of email addresses would be out of date before it was written. However, there are a couple of ways you can sometimes track down a mail address. One of them is through a UNIX command called Finger. You get onto the net, find yourself a command line interface, and type <finger address>. (You might try 'finger sue@s-sco.demon.co.uk'.) What you get back depends on what Finger finds as it rummages around the network routing looking for the address. You might get a 'Not Found' message or a 'Last Logged in' message. You might even get a text message back telling you all about the guy you have fingered, as some UNIX people like to put a small resumé in a text file (called a plan file) which gets sent to people who finger them. You might even get back the first line of something called the Project file, but this will be a rare occurrence, as UNIX users are too busy with political infighting about the superiority of one version of UNIX over another to get any real work done.

Finger often doesn't work as it's not always implemented on all systems for a variety of reasons, security being one of them, bad-tempered and paranoid network administrators being another. Some compilers of lists on the Internet put details of those lists into the plan file, so you get them when you finger the person's address. But don't depend on Finger to work all the time.

FAX gateways

Many email services offer a FAX gateway. This is a facility where you send electronic text to your Internet provider in the normal way, it's converted to a fax and then faxed. Fax gateways have their pros and cons. They don't (generally) operate for free – so you'll pay a premium on top of the call charge to the destination. To counter that, they can be useful for sending the odd fax when you're away from home, but the advent of the cheap fax modem makes most Fax-send gateways a little obsolete.

What is useful is a fax-to-email gateway. Your Auntie Flo, who knows nothing about modems, sends you a paper fax. It arrives in your mailbox and you call in and get it as electronically mailed text. Alas, fax-to-email gateways are still rare, as faxes aren't sent as text but as images. The conversion routine from fax to text is thus cumbersome and expensive to implement, and the character recognition software needed isn't 100% accurate. However, there are a number of companies selling virtual fax mailboxes. You take out a subscription and are given a fax number for the mailbox. Faxes arrive in the normal manner, and are stored until you call in and ask for them to be sent to you. You then set your computer's fax modem to receive mode, and wait for the fax to arrive.

Virtual fax mail is still a bit advanced, and not yet considered a part of the Internet email scene. Neither is it cheap enough for mass appeal. But it's extremely useful for the travelling salesman, or book author, and like all things electronic, will become more common as prices fall and Internet providers catch on. A London company called Business Space offers non-Internet Virtual Fax Mail. Talk to Jane Kirkham on 0171 917 9917 for details.

Finding the unfindable

You can often track down Internet users with WHOIS. You send email to mailserv@internic.net or any of the other whois servers with the command *whois xxx*. Here's part of the help file you'll get back when you send out a search message with the wrong syntax. But it's often better to get hold of email addresses by phoning the people concerned or by sending them a fax.

<OVERVIEW>

WHOIS is used to look up records in the main database. Each record has a "handle" (a unique identifier assigned to it), a name, a record type, and various other fields depending on the type of record.

To use WHOIS, simply type in your target string. The default action, unless directed otherwise with a keyword (e.g. "domain root"), is to do a very broad search, looking for matches to your target in many fields: handle, name, nicknames, hostname, net address, etc., and finding all record types.

WHOIS keywords fall into four categories: those that specify a FIELD to be searched, those that specify the TYPE of record to be found, those that modify the interpretation of the input or tell the type of output to produce, and those that are commands, such as HELP, QUIT, and so forth.

To tell WHOIS to restrict its search to ONLY a certain field in the database, there are the following three keywords (shown with their minimum abbreviation in all CAPS):

Examples:

HAndle or '!'	!sb65 or HA sb65
NAme or leading '.'	.borinski or NA borinski
Mailbox or contains '@'	stanb@host

Searching for X500 users

X500 is a global directory system defined by the International Standards Organization. It's used mainly by corporate bodies who have installed office automation systems with email systems, and provides the external directory system for those users. There's a utility on the 'Net called FRED which allows you to search X500 directories for a particular name, but it has to be said, as it's said in every other book about the Internet, that the best way of finding out someone's email address is to pick up the phone and ask them. If for some reason you can't do that, and you think the person concerned might be in an X500 directory, you can telnet to a fred server and enquire there. Alas, fred servers tend to be regional – despite X500 being a 'global' directory server – so telnetting to a USA based server may not always yield the correct results for a UK based user. Many Gopher servers are now carrying X500 directories, and using Gopher is an easier way of doing things. Fred servers are at wp.psi.com and wp2.psi.com, amongst other places, and you can telnet to them and log in as 'fred'. Type 'help' for a list of commands.

Favourite places

Some interesting email addresses from Seth Godin's book *Email Addresses of the Rich and Famous* – ISBN 0-201-40893-7 – reproduced with kind permission:

Al Gore – Vice President, USA
vice-president@whitehouse.gov

Anne McCaffrey, author
72007.1473@compuserve.com

Bill Clinton
president@whitehouse.gov

Bill Gates
billg@microsoft.com

Billy Idol, 'musician'
idol@phantom.com

Bob Hoskins, actor
75300.1313@compuserve.com

James Randi, magician
72740.456@compuserve.com

Santa Claus
santa@north.pole.org

Santa's elves
elves@north.pole.org

Terry Pratchett, 'writer'
tpratchett@unseen.demon.co.uk

The Clinton Administration
75300.3115@compuserve.com

Tom Clancy, author
tomclancy@aol.com

Most UK national newpapers, technical and computer magazines can now be contacted by email – their addresses are normally published in the small print alongside the publisher's address or under the byline for particular journalists. As yet you cannot contact most Members of Parliament or the Prime Minister by email, but there are rumours that this might happen 'soon'. The Queen doesn't have an email account, either, but is reputed to be saving up for one.

Favourite places – list servers (listservs)

You can get a complete listing of listservs by emailing ***listserv@bitnic.bitnet*** with the words 'list global' in the text.

Here's a tiny sample of what's available. Listservs come and go, so don't be disappointed if your favourite list is no longer working.

Animal rights
animal-rights-request@xanth.cs.odu.edu

Artificial life
alife-request@iuvax.cs.indiana.edu

British cars
british-cars-request@encore.com

Chaucer
listserv2siucvmb.siu.edu
(send: SUB CHAUCER <your real name here>)

Kites
kites-request@harvard.harvard.edu

More lists of mailing lists
mail-men-request@attunic.att.com

'Net stuff (ftp servers, lists and so on)
listserv%vmtecmex.bitnet@cunyvm.cuny.edu
(send: SUB NETSCOUT <your real name here>)

United Nations
listserv@indycms.iupui.edu

Vegetarian
listserv%gitvml.bitnet@cunyvm.cuny.edu
(send: SUB GRANOLA <your real name here>)

5 Network news

'Newsgroups
contain all of the
world's knowledge...'

As well as getting textual information from the 'Net via email and mail-lists you can also fill up your hard disk with information from Usenet. Usenet is really a large virtual bulletin board onto which any Tom, Dick and Harriet can post a message and Usenet therefore provides a wonderful global view of just what a complete waste of time man's endeavours on this planet really are. Messages may cover any topic and be posted onto any message base, but generally speaking messages in any given newsgroup will follow a particular topic. At least that's the theory, although there's much within Usenet topics which is decidedly 'off-topic'. Any message posted into a topic will be trundled around the world in a couple of days, or in some cases, hours.

Most Internet providers provide access to most Usenet groups, although many commercial sites remove access to groups containing material likely to be regarded as offensive. Many local bulletin board services now carry access to the Usenet too, but in some cases you're likely to find that you only have read-access – that is, you can't post messages or replies to messages, especially if you have a terminal-only connection.

Getting hold of Usenet

If your Internet provider supplies access to Usenet then you'll need a Usenet reader program to get at the information. These programs vary in their ability to make life difficult for the user. Many of them don't cater for capturing news to disk for perusal at a later date (thus saving on costs of running a dial-up line while you download, sort and read your news). Others have a clunky batch-driven system which attempts to provide offline facilities of some sort. The reason for this is simple. Until very recently the Internet was only for those who had a direct Ethernet connection, where you can spend as much time as you like plugged into the 'Net without running up phone charges. It's a problem which many American

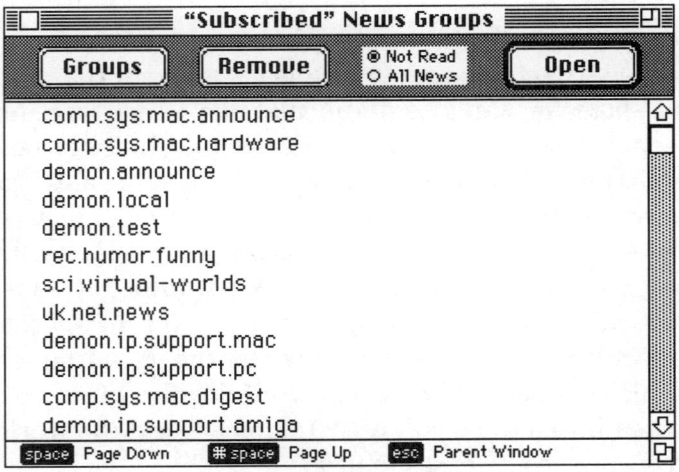

Figure 5.1 *Subscribed newsgroups. These are manually selected from a large list of all newsgroups in many news programs.*

software authors (and authors of American Internet books) haven't addressed, because dial-up access is still a minority sport in the Land of Plenty.

The best Usenet readers are hooked into your email facilities, so you can reply to a message either within the Usenet group or by personal email. Nearly all network news is delivered using a scheme called NNTP – Network News Transfer Protocol, and consequently you'll need an NNTP-savvy program to collect it from your provider. If you are using a terminal session, instead of a full TCP/IP connection, you can often get your news mailed to you as email. On some terminal systems you specify the groups you are interested in, and then go back in a couple of hours to collect the data which has been collected for you and saved into your mailbox. Again this is a clunky way of doing it, although better than nothing, and you do get the opportunity of reading your news with the phone disconnected – that is, offline.

Newsgroup contents

Newsgroups contain all of the world's knowledge. The great disadvantage is that this knowledge is filtered down through the minds of geeks, know-it-alls, journalists, computer-bigots, religious fundamentalists and techno-wibblers, and you have to do a lot of panning to find just a little gold.

Newsgroups are divided into hierarchies and their title is thus supposed to be descriptive of their contents. Anything beginning with SCI should contain topics bearing some resemblance to scientific matters, REC is recreational, SOC is social, and so on. There are also a lot of regional groups, where Germans can speak German, or at least write messages to each other in German, Finns can write in Finnish, and Americans can have a stab at English. You'll also find Russian newsgroups full of what appears to be random gibberish, for which you will need a program capable of decoding Cyrillic characters. The result is random Russian gibberish. Similar sentiments may be expressed about Japanese newsgroups.

There are any numbers of ALT newsgroups too, where ALT stands for 'alternative'. Here you can pick up all sorts of things, many of which will not respond either to medical treatment or to

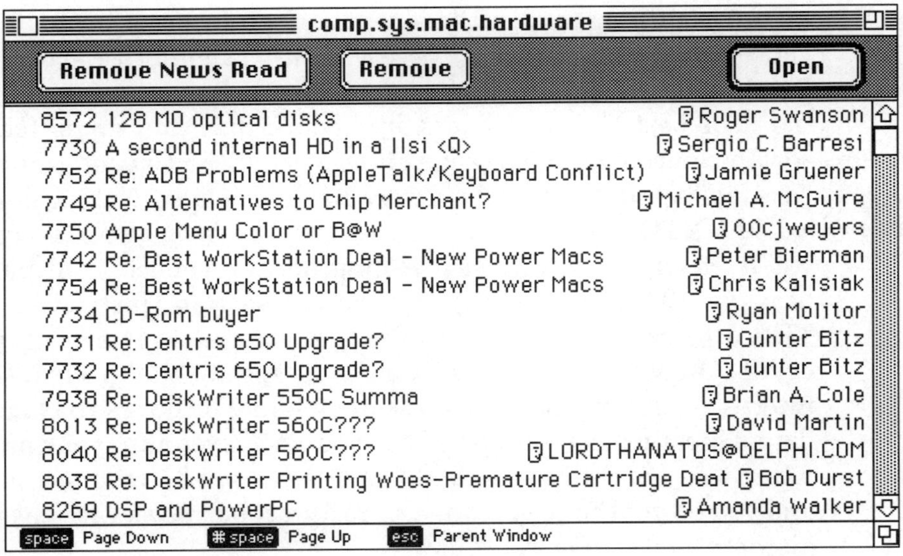

Figure 5.2 *Contents of a newsgroup. Each line is an individual message.*

localized anti-pornography legislation. You get hold of image files from Usenet groups by using the UUdecode or BinHex decoders mentioned in Chapter 4.

It's the 'uninhibited' nature of the Internet in general, and Usenet in particular, which is causing the hairs on the necks of UK Government ministers to stand up. Already the media has latched on to the fact that there are images and messages in many of the ALT Usenet groups which are deemed unsuitable for public consumption in this country, and it's very likely that the next few years will bring in some sort of knee-jerk legislation to limit access to these feeds in the UK. The only real way that this can be done is to threaten Internet providers with the crime of distributing pornography, which will result in many of the Usenet groups being pulled from general distribution. When that happens it will be a sad day for the anti-censorship brigade, and a bonus for the Thought Police. In the meantime you can gain access to most of the Usenet groups, most of the time, through most of the Internet providers in this country.

Getting your hands dirty with Usenet

The actuality of Usenet is simple – you join a newsgroup and download or read online the messages it contains. If you feel sufficiently moved you hit a key, and your computer presents you with a text editor into which you compose your message and then hit the send key. Your witty and brilliant reply then appears in the newsgroup and is there the next time you log on. (The actual mechanism of Usenet programs varies, so don't worry too much if you are using a different editor to compose your Usenet replies to the one you would use for your email.)

Many Usenet messages seem to be entirely constructed of the text from the previous message, preceded by a > sign. This is a function of some text editor programs, where you click an on-screen button marked 'Reply' and the editor constructs the reply message headers but adds in the complete text of the message to which you are replying. This makes it very convenient for you, but a pain in the butt for everyone else who has to read the complete text of a message dozens of times over. The problem gets worse when Internet geeks, intent on making some facile point, will not only copy the entire message, but the ten-line signature of the guy who sent it in the first place. This makes sure that out of the 30 megabytes of Usenet stuff you've downloaded at great cost, only ten bits of it is of any real interest. The rest is repeats of messages and signatures. So, use your editor with care and sense, and watch for that copying facility. It can get out of hand. And keep your signature (called a 'sig' in geek-speak) to three lines or less. It all helps keep the tedium of free speech to a minimum.

Some newsgroups are 'moderated', which means that you can't post to them directly. A 'moderator' is someone who is egocentric enough to believe they should operate a closed newsgroup, and limit or control what appears in it. To send mail to a moderated news group you mail the moderator directly, who then decides whether what you have to say carries any virtue and includes it if it doesn't.

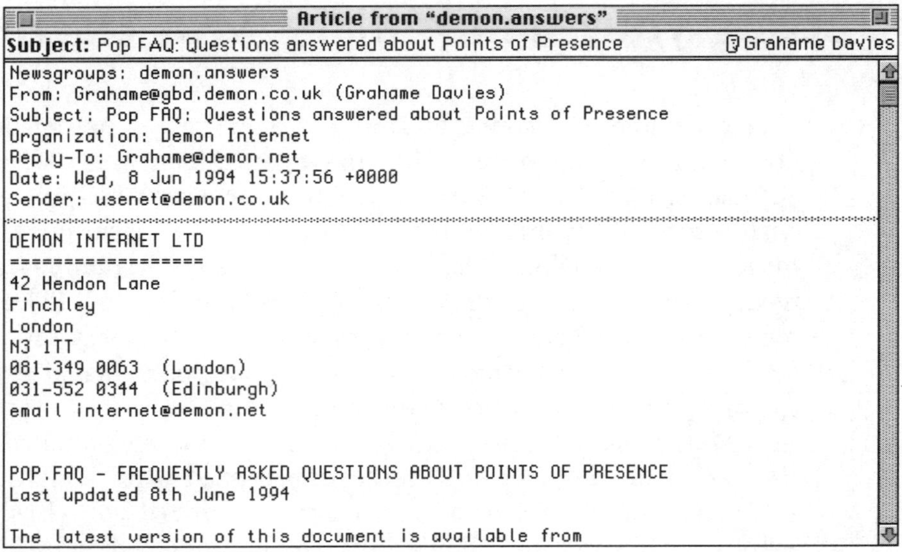

Article from "demon.answers"

Subject: Pop FAQ: Questions answered about Points of Presence   Grahame Davies

```
Newsgroups: demon.answers
From: Grahame@gbd.demon.co.uk (Grahame Davies)
Subject: Pop FAQ: Questions answered about Points of Presence
Organization: Demon Internet
Reply-To: Grahame@demon.net
Date: Wed, 8 Jun 1994 15:37:56 +0000
Sender: usenet@demon.co.uk

DEMON INTERNET LTD
==================
42 Hendon Lane
Finchley
London
N3 1TT
081-349 0063  (London)
031-552 0344  (Edinburgh)
email internet@demon.net


POP.FAQ - FREQUENTLY ASKED QUESTIONS ABOUT POINTS OF PRESENCE
Last updated 8th June 1994

The latest version of this document is available from
```

Figure 5.3 *Contents of a message. You can respond either by mail, or directly to the newsgroup with many news/email packages.*

Net etiquette

There is a spurious form of fascist control on the Internet, imposed by cyber-idealists and regulated by its denizens. 'Netiquette' demands that you use lower case for all public mail (upper case is translated as SHOUTING!) and that you shouldn't use more than three lines for your signature as it 'uses up disk space'. These rules (and others) seem extremely petty once you're plugged into the Internet, especially when you see some of the blasphemous and obscene messages posted by users, and mind-blowingly inconsequential stuff posted by religious evangelists. It seems that while you can inform the world that Elvis Presley is not only God, but is alive and well and will be signing books at MacDonuts on Thursday, you can't use upper case for the text of a message.

Strange also, that the Internet community which prides itself so much on its supposed freedom should choose to impose any limits at all, but then anarchy can only work properly if it's correctly controlled. Whether you subscribe to Netiquette is up to you. But use upper case incautiously and all of the spotty dog's-breath students sitting with their feet up at the American taxpayers' expense will send you mail grumbling about your wild excursion into the unknown.

Other Netiquette inconsequences include sniffy comments about the Internet being used for 'commerce', and wildly out-of-order comments by UK based administrators of the JANET system (Joint Academic Network). One of these chaps recently posted a message complaining of recreational use of JANET by British people, mentioning that while it's OK for American students to use JANET, we Brits aren't allowed access other than for research. Seems reasonable, when you consider it's we Brits who are paying for it.

Newsgroup distribution

Remember that whatever you send to a Usenet group is splashed all over the world in a matter of hours, and can be and often is reproduced without permission or payment, so be careful of what you say. However, there are ways you can limit distribution of your postings. If you put a line in your message header thus, you'll limit distribution to the USA only:

Distribution: usa

There are huge numbers of distribution limiters, so most people don't bother with them, mainly because they don't always work. But you can limit your postings to just the UK with the UK suffix, so try that if you don't want the whole world to comment on your writing abilities. If you have a half-decent editor on your system you'll find that there's a 'distribution' box which pops up with a pick list of all the distribution limiters. If you're using DOS then you'll do it manually, at the moment. And if you are using one of the American based Shareware Usenet programs you'll find it difficult to set distribution parameters automatically, as all Americans believe that all communication should go worldwide. 'Communication is Knowledge', they say, in much the same way as they sold us chewing gum and hula hoops.

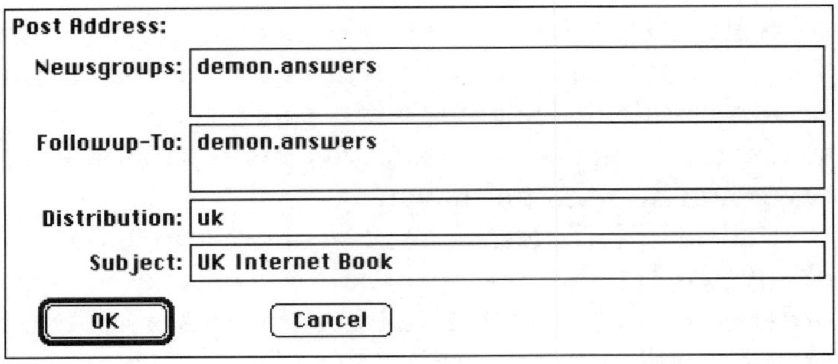

Figure 5.4 *You should be able to set the distribution of your newsgroup postings. This one will only appear in UK newsgroups.*

New newsgroups

New groups appear on Usenet almost by the hour. Many of them will have little or no consequence to you (or anyone else) and you won't want them eating up space on your computer. Your NNTP news program will either tell you that a new group has been created, or will provide a clicky-button which you can press to show all the new groups which have sprung up since you last checked. Many DOS based news programs run a check for new groups either on demand or when you start up your connection. In every case you'll have a command which lets you join, or ignore, each new group.

Every so often, say once a month for newsgroup freaks, you'll want to grab a complete list of all newsgroups, and then spend a week formatting it up as a nice text document which you can pin on the bathroom wall. You've then got a huge list of newsgroups which you can browse through at leisure, selecting target groups to add to your personal list.

If you're a modem user and you want to try this then make sure you do it a time when you can afford the resultant phone bill. Many news programs not only download the complete list of newsgroups but sort them alphabetically too, and they will quite happily do this while your modem is sitting on the line eating up your non-disposable income. Despite this warning, most Internet freaks have huge and complete lists of newsgroups lying around like confetti, which shows just why the telecomms providers are

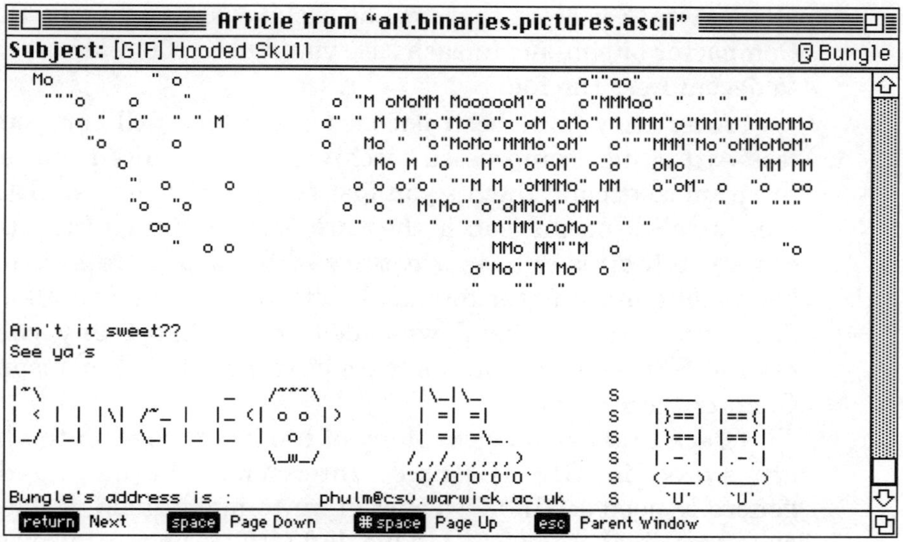

Figure 5.5 *An exotic 'sig' made of ASCII characters.*

starting to get interested in the Internet. In principle you can join and leave newsgroups at will; in reality your ability to do this will be limited or enhanced by the software you're using to provide access. Some providers keep an up-to-date list which can be downloaded very quickly but you may or may not be able to use this with your news reader directly.

Yes, but is it Art?

Many newsgroups provide binary files of images, artistic or otherwise, and there are a number of techniques used over the Internet to get these files into standard messages. The most common is to encode a binary file such as an image file into an ASCII representation of itself with a program called UUencode, and to use UUdecode to bring the file back to binary. It can then be decompressed if need be, and run on your computer. Quite often these files turn out to be compressed archives, which for PC users means that they will be compressed using PKZip or a similar alternative. For Macs they will be archives created using Stuffit or Compactor or similar. In each case you'll need the relevant software to decompress the file.

After they have been decoded some files will turn out to be 'self-extracting compressed archives'. These need no external program to expand them – you just run them if they are DOS EXE files, or click on an icon if they are Mac or Amiga files. In many cases you'll already have a battery of file decompressors if you've been using a computer for any length of time, and in all cases all decompressors can be downloaded from almost any computer-centric FTP site. (If you don't understand what that means, read Chapter 8 on FTP.)

Back to those images. Many of the image files on the Internet are stored in GIF (Graphics Interchange Format) and you'll generally need a GIF viewer program to make them visible. There are a wealth of other formats too, but GIF is the most used and you can always find a GIF viewer for your particular computer on the Internet.

Listserv

Listserv groups are slightly different to Usenet groups. You send a mail message to the group's email address, and your message gets sent to everyone on the list, if it's set up that way. Everyone else's mail gets sent to you in return. (On some systems mail only gets sent between originating and replying authors, and consenting adults.)

Listserv is a great way of generating mail to yourself, but beware the cost of downloading a hundred mail messages over a dial-up link. Watch out too if you're a CompuServe user. Harry Gard, the man who invented CompuServe in 1969, decreed that users of that service would pay an extra fee for receiving Internet mail. Consequently you'll go bankrupt the day that 4000 messages concerning Life, the Universe, and KY Jelly come flooding into your CompuServe mailbox. (You can get a complete list of listserv servers by sending 'list global' to listserv@bitnic.educom.edu. Don't send your ten-line signature, and don't expect a rapid reply.)

When you find a listserv which you think is worthy of your razor-sharp intellect, you send a subscribe message:

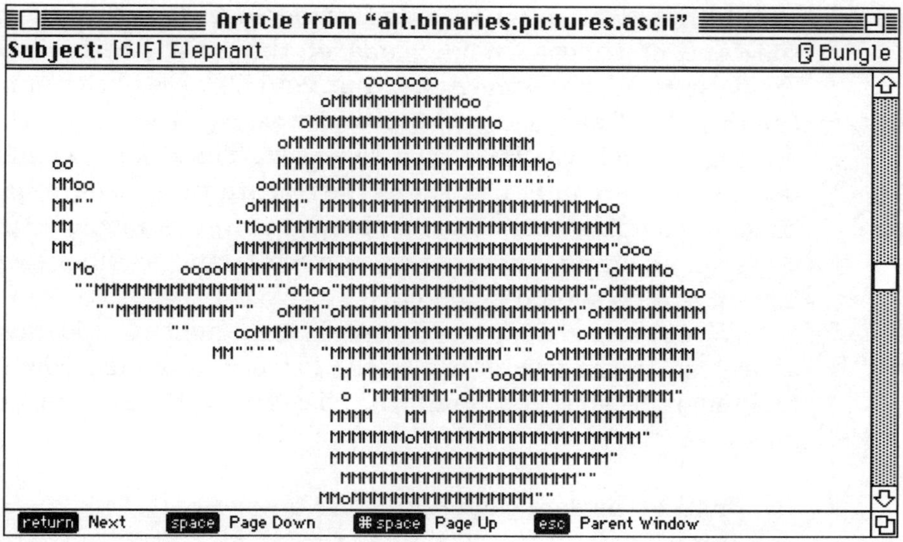

Figure 5.6 *ASCII elephant, from the alt.binaries.ascii newsgroup.*

mail to: listserv@ames.arc.nasa.gov

---

subscribe frequent-flyer name

Don't send <name> – it won't bring you any large cheques. And use your own real name, not your email address. (The listserv picks up your email address from your mail header.) You can abbreviate 'subscribe' to 'sub' if you like beaming non-human-readable messages around the world.

The listserv address is actually 'frequent-flyer@ames.arc.nasa.gov' but you are sending your request for mail to the listserv computer. You now wait until you get your first 5000 mail messages, or you start sending mail to the group:

Mail to: frequent-flyer@ames.arc.nasa.gov

Hi Guys,

Did you hear the one about the Sopwith Camel and the Fokker?

– but it might be better to get a few messages first so you can judge the tone of things. In fact, one of the least benign aspects of 'Netiquette' is that some newsgroup contributors like to jump down the throats of new users who post messages, especially if they post messages which say 'Hi – I'm a new user'. These benign and literate people (who are only fascists in their spare time) tend to put first-time users off as part of some obscure power struggle, so previous remarks about sitting around for a while and watching what the Grown-ups do should be noted.

When subscribing to listservs your mail should always be addressed to the group, not to the listserv, although when you've had enough you can mail the listserv with an 'unsubscribe' message:

> mail to: listserv@ames.arc.nasa.gov
>
> ---
>
> signoff frequent-flyer

You can also mail the listserv with a demand for help, and if you send 'info ?' you should get a list of available documentation back. 'Help' will bring you the help files.

Look out for the SET commands available on your favourite listserv. 'SET frequent-flyer digest' will bundle all your replies up into a daily report. Not all SET commands are available on all listservs, so check out the help files.

Other useful commands are:

SET xxx NOACK, which stops the blessed thing returning your own mail to you as an acknowledgement.

SET xxx NOMAIL, which stops mail temporarily.

SET xxx MAIL starts it again.

The listserv system shows up the pitfalls of trying to communicate with three million people from your back bedroom. Listserv is quite a dumb process, and you'll get lots of messages from some servers saying that such-and-such people who were once on the list are no longer reachable. You might also fall unsuspecting into a moderated list, where the moderator used to be a Personnel Manager, and doesn't let your messages into the list until you've been a subscriber for a year, just so you know your place. And some moderators are Network Nazis, and won't let you into the list unless you agree entirely with what they have to say, and sign a Non Disclosure Agreement (NDA).

To complicate matters some apparently private lists are mirrored in Usenet groups. You then find that, where you mistakenly believed you were replying to just a couple of hundred people, your mother/boss/publisher finds you plastered publicly all over Alt.Hamster.Eating, or worse. Quite often it's the newsgroups which find themselves targets of outraged moral stances taken up by journalists paid to be outraged, and it's not rare to see out-of-context Usenet messages plastered all over the US tabloids. So if eating hamsters is your bag, at least use an alias. Don't use sue@s-sco.demon.co.uk – it's already taken.

The one thing to remember about both listserv and newsgroups is not to open your electronic mouth unless you have something worth communicating. If everyone on the Internet followed that credo then two-thirds of mail-lists and newsgroups would dry up overnight and there would be dancing in the middle lane of the Digital Superhighway, when it finally arrives.

The curse of ROT13

What you want to read on an Internet newsgroup or mail-list is up to you. There is no censorship on the 'Net, other than at a local level, because there's no single governing body. As mentioned previously, the ROT13 encryption scheme is used to protect more sensitive individuals from the content of some of the newsgroups, but in practice all this serves to do is to flag the message as being especially suitable for the sexually curious or hamster-vores. In the UK we are much less open about sexual matters than in other countries and you may decide that you don't want your 13-year-old daughter (or son) getting hold of some of the material that's available. This is a real problem for many parents and at the moment there is no solution, other than to try to be reasonable. The general reaction to computer based communication of sexual matters is to ban it, which simply serves to push it underground, where it reappears covertly in school playgrounds. It's far better to talk it through with your children before making Draconian rules about what they can and can't access on Daddy's computer.

Some half-decent Usenet groups

Most of the stuff on Usenet is of limited interest to UK users, simply because the vast part of it originates in the USA, where different value systems apply. You'll doubtless find your own level in these groups but for newcomers there's news.announce. newusers. News.answers is worth looking at (allegedly) although rec.humor.funny, which is mentioned in all the other Internet books as being riotously amusing, is about as funny as a heap of dingo's kidneys, as far as this scribbler is concerned. If you want real humour (with two u's) then join alt.zen where there are often bizarre clashes between materialistic Zen Masters armed with computers, and nerds who have met someone whose best friend knows a guy who once read *Zen and the Art of Motorcycle Maintenance* – over someone else's shoulder.

Favourite places – Usenet

Here's a list of selected newsgroups, which might, or might not, be of some interest. If not there's 40,000 more available, at the last count. You can get lists of groups from various places, including news.announce.newusers. Look out too, for the Clarinet (clari) newsgroups, which contain real news from around the world. Your Internet provider may not provide them as there's a cost implication, although you can subscribe to them personally with a credit card.

Newsgroups

comp.society.cu.digest
A moderated group – The underground Computer Digest.

misc.misc
A miscellany of miscellany. Contains much of little interest.

misc.kids.computer
Sprogs and pooters come away...

misc.consumers
Consumer topics of an American kind.

rec.scuba
Think or thwim.

cern.ski.club
Off-piste particle physics from the Swiss Atom-Smashers.

soc.women
Non-male topics.

talk.bizarre
Aliens from the planet Thrarg meet Marks & Spencer Man.

alt.paranormal
Things that go BMP in the night.

alt.sex
Sex is what the middle class put their coal in.

alt.ascii.art
Pictures made of letters, intriguingly daft.

alt.comedy.british
Comments on us, by foreigners.

demon.adverts
Sell your grannie at half price.

(Demon also carry many useful UK computer support groups. Grab a full list from your News server for details.)

6 Telnet

'You can log into
NASA databases
and pickup info on
Shuttle launches...'

Do you remember those old Star Trek movies, where Captain Kirk would beam down to another planet, blast a few harmless life-forms, and then be back home in time to nibble Uhuru's communicator? Telnet is a bit like that – it enables you to pop 'into' the computer of your choice, perform a few miracles, and then pop back home with only minimum damage to your dilithium crystals. Telnet is yet another bit of client software which you can use to log on to remote computers, and perform tasks as though you are sitting at the remote computer itself.

There are a few conditions though. You'd find it difficult to run a Windows program over telnet, because telnet doesn't understand the new-fangled personal computer thingies, although you could telnet into the computer used to control the Hubble space telescope – because you don't need anything as complicated as Windows to run multi-billion-dollar space projects. So telnet is a bit like all the other bits of the Internet: it's OK if you can find a use for it, a waste

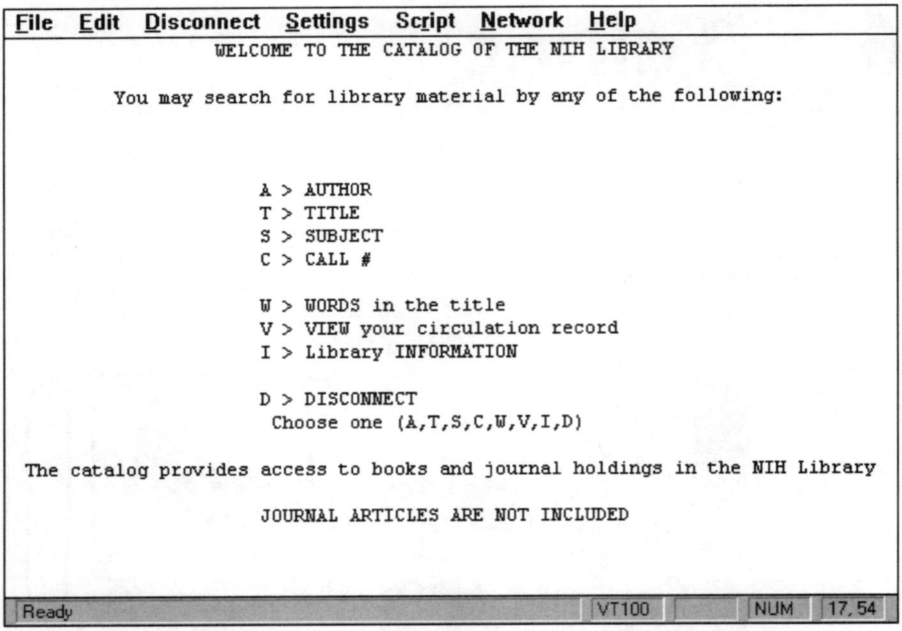

Figure 6.1 *Telnetting to the National Institutes of Health Library in the USA.*

of hard disk space if you can't.

Fortunately there's no shortage of places on the Internet you can telnet into. Want to order a book (this one maybe)? Telnet to books.com and you can search book titles for the one you want. The commercial company (remember the 'com' suffix) that runs the service will also take your order for the book and mail it to you the same day. Want to rummage around NASA's database of extra-galactic objects? The same applies, although you can't as yet order black holes on your credit card. There are too many telnet sites to list in this section of the book, and you'll have to trust me when I say that telnet is remarkably useful, once you get the hang of all the nerdy stuff you need to get it going. It's telnet which gives you basic access to many of the Internet's secrets, such as Archie, Gopher, Internet Relay Chat and live backgammon sessions.

It pays to get the hang of telnet, because having the ability to run programs on other people's computers is a great asset, and the joke about controlling space telescopes from that heap of tin you are pleased to call a computer is in fact a reality.

What you need for telnet

You need a telnet client installed on your computer, that's what. If you use the services of an Internet provider, you might be able to use the telnet client installed on his computer. But in either case you'll also need a 'terminal emulator' – which is a long word for a piece of software which makes your exotic personal computer look like a boring old character based terminal. Yes folks, UNIX systems still talk to users via dumb terminals, so please don't snigger through the rest of this chapter. But which terminal software? And just what is a terminal anyway?

A terminal is something which, in its most basic form, takes in and spits out computer information and displays it on a screen or printout. In its most advanced form a terminal can also take in human input and convert it into something computers understand. The earliest terminals were simple solenoid-operated printers, and as electric keyboards became available they were tagged onto printers to give them an input/output capability. Old-timers will remember the 'TeleType' printers which used to print up the BBC's football results on screen. If you're under 25 you won't have a clue what I'm talking about.

Despite being old technology, terminals are still used in the UNIX world because UNIX was developed to talk to human beings through dumb character based interfaces. Terminals also happen to be cheaper than personal computers, which is why there are still vast numbers of them around in the commercial and academic world.

Like everything else in the computer world, there are various standards for terminals – a standard in this case being something that one manufacturer hopes to foist upon all the others, and the most common standards are Digital Equipment's DEC VT100/VT102 emulations, and TeleType (TTY). TTY terminal emulation is exceedingly simple, and is the preferred method of getting around, but most UNIX boxes expect to see a slightly more exotic terminal emulation. VT100/102, or derivatives VT220 and VT320, are all used somewhere on the Internet, and you'll need a program on your computer that can provide these emulations. If you trip over a remote system running on a large IBM system, you'll probably find you need IBM 3101 emulation or even 3270, although it's surprising what you can get away with if you try VT100 on everything.

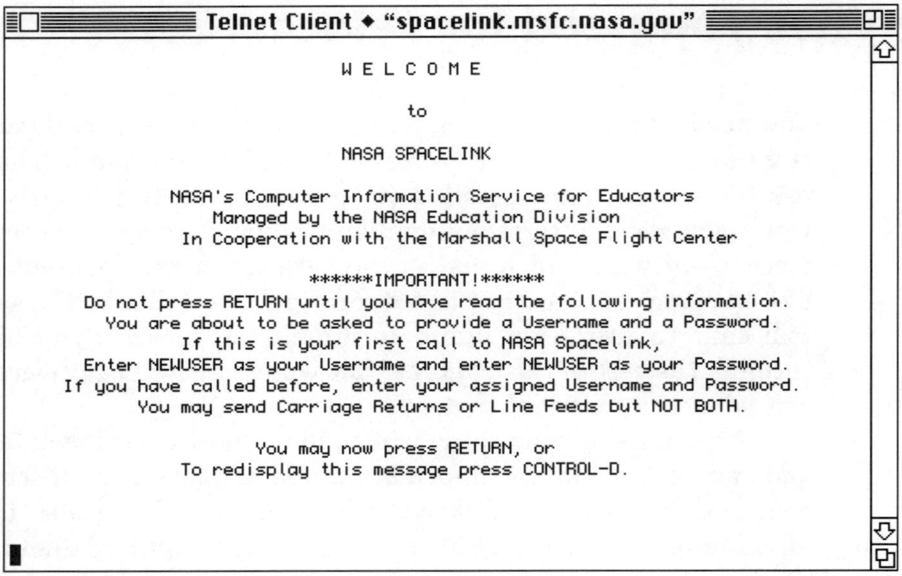

Figure 6.2 *The Nasa Spacelink Service via telnet.*

Don't forget that your terminal emulation program needs to sit on top of all the other stuff you need for Internet working. You still need your transport system (TCP/IP), your modem handler (SLIP or PPP) and your telnet client software. You can't just use a terminal emulator on its own to hook into the Internet, unless you are going through a third-party gateway such as a dial-up bulletin board.

Once you've grasped this annoying fact, you can set up your terminal emulator and get hooked up to the Internet. Unfortunately there are no hard and fast rules about setting up your terminal software, but a good place to start is with VT100 emulation, which will get you into most places. The rule is – if in doubt revert to either TTY or VT100.

Telnet commands

Telnet servers have their own series of commands. Once you're into one you'll need to get out, and the best way to do that is to type 'quit'. If this doesn't terminate your connection to the server then try sending CTRL] (hold down the CTRL key and then press the

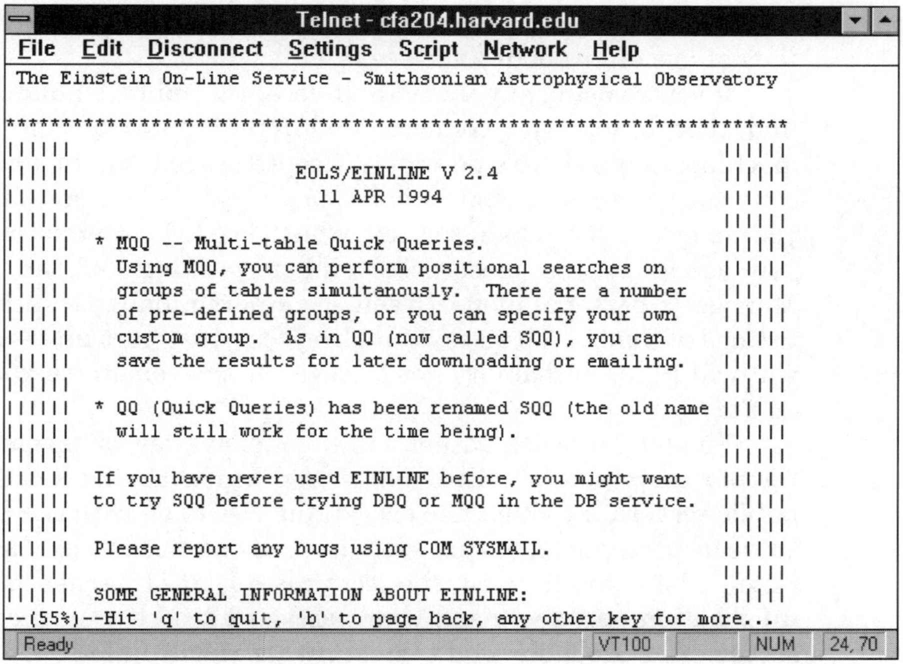

Figure 6.3 *The Smithsonian Astrophysical Laboratory (login as einline).*

square bracket sign). This is the telnet escape sequence, and it should drop you back to the telnet> prompt, where you can then type 'quit'. If it doesn't, try CTRL D, or CTRL C. Other logout sequences exist, and the best way to discover them is at first hand. If your terminal has a 'log to disk' facility or a 'scroll-back buffer' then you can use these to grab the data on the screen from the remote service and save it for later perusal.

Other telnet secrets

Telnet seems impenetrable to users of modern personal computers. This is because it *is* impenetrable, and no amount of reading books will be a substitute for telnetting around and making a nuisance of yourself. The trick is to log in to your Internet provider and type telnet <sitename>, or fire up your telnet client. A good basic telnet site to start with is books.com. Order a book while you're in there – they arrive after about four weeks.

If you're using any sort of half-decent terminal emulator you'll find that it lets you connect to different ports on the remote machine. Again there's no widely accepted regime about which port connects you to what, but in many cases logging into one port gives you access to the public service, whilst logging into another gives you access to the most secret inner workings of the System Manager's personal diary. If you see a port number mentioned in listings of telnet addresses then always try that port first – because you will in all probability get thrown off the remote server if you don't.

Finally there's a rather more complex way of logging in to remote servers. It's called rlogin, and tends not be available on public servers, although like everything else to do with the Internet there are exceptions to that statement. If you need to use help with rlogin then you'll need the services of an Internet guru, as information about you and your password are kept on the remote server. You probably won't come across rlogin unless you have a corporate account on a server, and if you do then the best place to go for advice about how to use it is the System Manager's office.

Slow servers

Like all Internet processes telnet can seem extremely slow at times. You type in a command, the screen starts to display text ... and suddenly stops. The only advice, especially if you're paying online or telephone charges, is to log out from slow telnet sessions, and try again later. It's often the case that telnet servers slow down drastically when under load from the other 655 000 users logged in, and your only recourse is to disconnect. The speed of telnet sessions also depends on the load placed on all the various bits of the routers, cables and other bits of elec-trickery which make up the Internet, so the best advice for maximizing throughput on telnet or FTP sessions is to use the Internet during off-peak hours, as far as possible. You can get a fast session to most USA servers from the UK between 7:00–12:00 hrs GMT, as the USA is six or more hours behind us. Some UK Internet users also claim faster results after midnight, UK time.

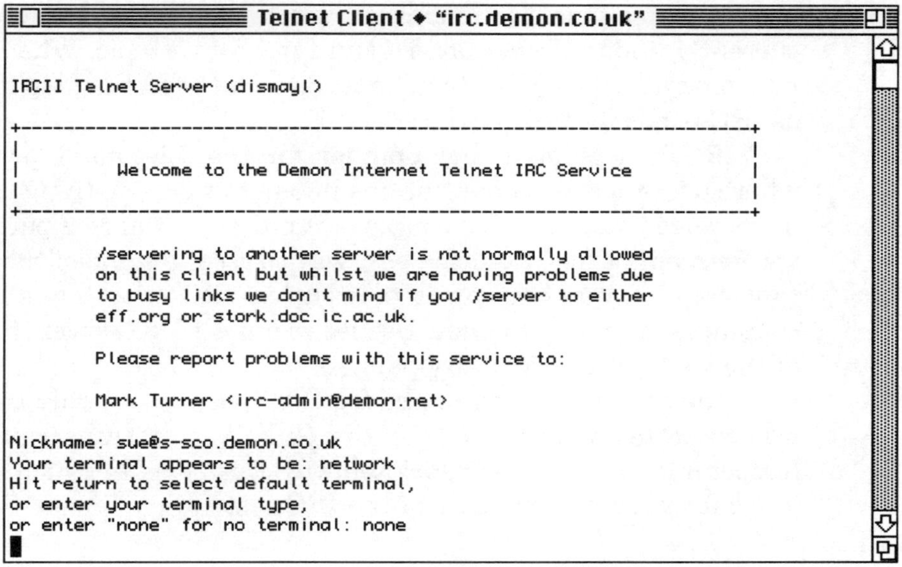

Figure 6.4 *An Internet Relay Chat server via telnet. This is the only screen we could find suitable for family viewing...*

Go to the talkies

Telnet opens up lots of avenues to the Internet rummager. One of the most futile is Internet Relay Chat, a sort of electronic river of garbage into which you empty the trashcan of your own personality. IRC is the place to find nerds, geeks, blasphemers, neo-nazis, rebels without a cause, causes without rebels – and computer journalists. In short it's an uncontrolled moving ribbon of human detritus. Consequently it's much loved by adolescents with terminal acne (a joke there somewhere) or by older folk with hairs growing on the palms of their hands. No, don't check – it's the first sign of madness. IRC was designed by a Finn, presumably because there's nothing to do in Finland during the long winters. It's a bit like Iceland, which has the highest rate of computer literacy in the world because it's too cold to do anything except breed and muck about with computers. There's a similar joke about Norway, where family trees apparently don't have any forks in them.

You get into IRC by telnetting to an IRC server. A good UK one is irc.demon.co.uk. You'll be asked for a nickname, and when that's been accepted type /LIST. This will scroll up a list of available topics currently under discussion. To join type /join #topic. When you've had enough, type /QUIT to get out, fast. But read the help file first, as IRC is not for novices.

IRC is a great money spinner for the telecomms providers, where users spend an hour on the phone to say something that can be handled by speech in a couple of minutes. If you're a parent and you're reading this, then the best way to recoup some of the money that your 12-year-old son is blowing on IRC is to buy shares in communications companies. Usenet group Alt.IRC serves the needs of the well-heeled and hairy-palmed.

One of the great triumphs for IRC (perhaps its only triumph) was to act as a news feed for the Gulf War. A transcript of the happenings is on the disk enclosed with this book, in which you can judge for yourself the value of the IRC system.

Telnet file transfers

There are any number of terminal based telnet services around. If you have a CompuServe account you can telnet to ***compuserve.com***. You can also use your normal ZMODEM, XMODEM and other file transfer protocols at some telnet sites, because all telnet is doing is providing the link service between you and the remote system. And you can generally use your dedicated front end software over telnet – for instance, you can use CompuServe's WinCim software over telnet, instead of going in via a dial-up line. However, your ordinary terminal software may not be able to communicate over TCP/IP, which is the transport protocol going on underneath telnet. This is because most UK based communications programs like to talk over modems and you'll need a TCP/IP, compliant terminal program to make ZMODEM (or other asynchronous file transfer protocols) work over telnet.

Hytelnet

Hytelnet is an attempt to bring the Graphical User Interface to boring old character based terminals. It's also a neat way to find out about telnet and telnet sites. You log in to a Hytelnet site and follow the prompts. Use the cursor arrows to move up to the <highlighted> options and press Enter. Hytelnet will bring up the page with the information on it. The place to start your search for interesting sites is a Hytelnet server such ***access.usask.ca***. Hytelnet has been overshadowed by recent developments such as the World Wide Web, but is mentioned here for old time's sake.

Telnet services

Telnet is an important part of the Internet, because it lets you do real work. You can log into the Library of Congress and check out almost any book or author, you can log into the NASA databases and pickup info on Shuttle launches. More than a thousand other databases are available for browsing.

You can also play Backgammon or GO in realtime against a human opponent by telnetting to a server and getting stuck in, and playing games over the Internet is a favourite way for American students to spend taxpayers' money on an 'education'. The most notorious sapper of tax-dollars is the Multi-User Domain, or MUD. MUD is a game where you solve problems – such as how to pick up the jewels without waking up your tutor. You can also meet other telnetters inside the domain, pretending to be wizards, or dwarves – hence the multi-user tag. MUDs are such attractive places to be that there is now real concern about students junking their academic career in favour of typing:

<go left>
<pick up>
<put down>
<vaporize>

and so on.

There are vast numbers of online games available at ***lambda.parc.xerox.com*** (port 8888), including online chess games. You can find out more by loitering around the ***rec.games*** newsgroups, which carry crazed messages from gamesters stuck at the first post.

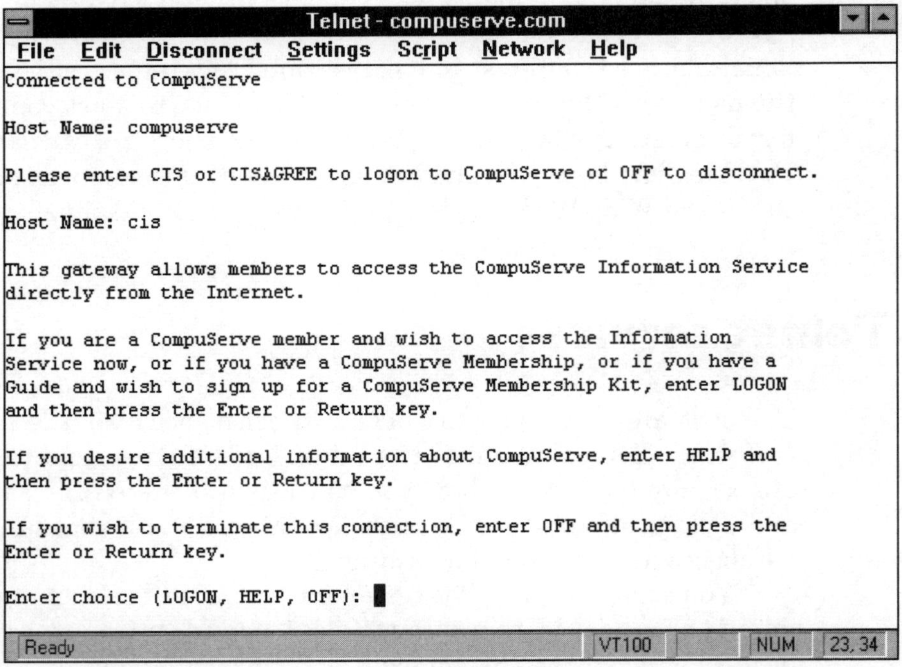

Figure 6.5 *Accessing CompuServe via telnet. Most of the larger online services now support telnet access.*

Favourite places – telnet

access.usask.ca
Login as hytelnet. Site contains details of many telnet resources.

Books.com
Search for authors or book titles. Shipping to the UK takes about four weeks and costs less than four dollars.

Colorada Alliance of Research Libraries (CARL)
pac.carl.org, login as pac.

eve.assumption.edu port 5000
Takes you to dragon.mud, the text based adventure game. Watch those phone bills.

Internet Relay Chat
The UK server is at irc.demon.co.uk. Another lives at prof.jpl.nasa.gov, which is based at the Jet Propulsion Lab in California.

Library of Congress
locis.loc.gov
Catalogue to the biggest library in the world. Access is often limited for non-USA calls, but it is possible to get in, from 9 a.m. to 9 p.m. Eastern time.

Library at Dartford College
library.dartford.edu.
Includes lots of Shakespeare. Busy site when we tried it.

Merit Network
hermes.merit.edu
Gateway to Michigan's regional net. Lets you into many US online services, including SprintNet and CompuServe. Useful if you're travelling out of the UK and need to get your CompuServe mail from an Internet workstation. Other good gateways for rummaging include Washington University at wugate.wustl.edu.

Nasa News
spacelink.msfc.nasa.gov
You'll need to leave your name (register) to get access to lots of NASA info, including details of Shuttle schedules. Other good space places are ersin.esa.it for details of European Space Agency doings.

Scrabble
next2.cas.muohio.edu port 777
Online Scrabble.

gopher.netsys.com – login as enews for Electronic NewsStand.

bbs.noplace.com – No Place Like Home BBS.

liberty.uc.wlu.ed – login: lawlib.

ds.internic.net – login: wais, for InterNIC Directory of Directories.

archie.doc.ic.ac.uk – login: archie for Archie use via telnet.

7 Uncle Archie

'Results can take up to three days to arrive...'

After six chapters of getting slowly used to fighting with UNIX, you're probably ready for Archie. Archie is a tool that helps you find information on the Internet, and like all tools on the Internet its usefulness depends on the ability of human beings to order data into neat and tidy piles. (If it's not in the tidy pile, then Archie can't find it.)

Archie has been described as a card index of Internet files, which is a bit of a misnomer. Archie is more like that deaf old bat you employed 20 years ago as a secretary, and haven't yet had the heart to fire. You tell Archie to go and find a file, and then it comes back with lots of not quite the right information. Archie is only one of the search methods available on the Internet, and like most character based interfaces, it's looking more shabby with each day that passes. If you prefer to use Gopher to search for your data then you can bypass Archie for much of your rummaging, but it's included here to prevent book reviewers from shooting me down in

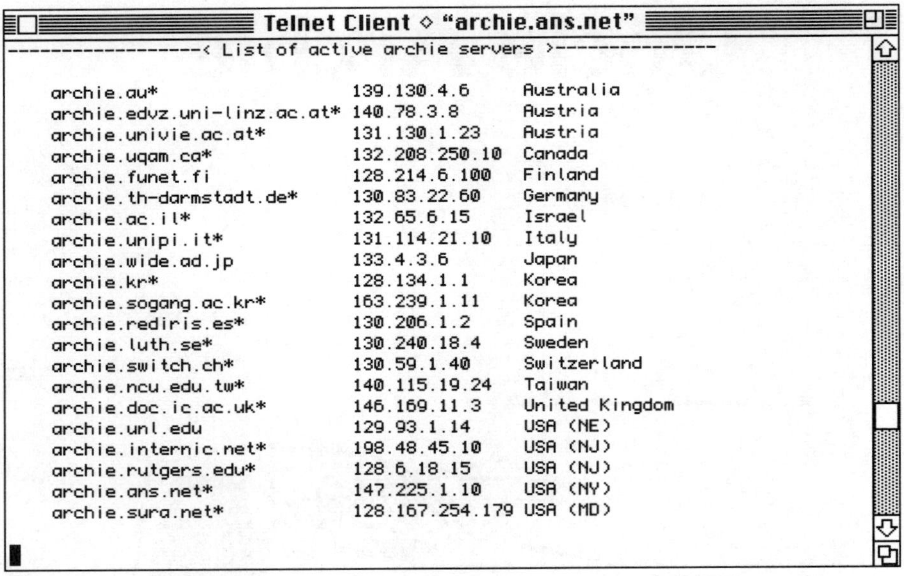

```
Telnet Client ◇ "archie.ans.net"
-----------------< List of active archie servers >---------------

    archie.au*                     139.130.4.6      Australia
    archie.edvz.uni-linz.ac.at*    140.78.3.8       Austria
    archie.univie.ac.at*           131.130.1.23     Austria
    archie.uqam.ca*                132.208.250.10   Canada
    archie.funet.fi                128.214.6.100    Finland
    archie.th-darmstadt.de*        130.83.22.60     Germany
    archie.ac.il*                  132.65.6.15      Israel
    archie.unipi.it*               131.114.21.10    Italy
    archie.wide.ad.jp              133.4.3.6        Japan
    archie.kr*                     128.134.1.1      Korea
    archie.sogang.ac.kr*           163.239.1.11     Korea
    archie.rediris.es*             130.206.1.2      Spain
    archie.luth.se*                130.240.18.4     Sweden
    archie.switch.ch*              130.59.1.40      Switzerland
    archie.ncu.edu.tw*             140.115.19.24    Taiwan
    archie.doc.ic.ac.uk*           146.169.11.3     United Kingdom
    archie.unl.edu                 129.93.1.14      USA (NE)
    archie.internic.net*           198.48.45.10     USA (NJ)
    archie.rutgers.edu*            128.6.18.15      USA (NJ)
    archie.ans.net*                147.225.1.10     USA (NY)
    archie.sura.net*               128.167.254.179  USA (MD)
```

Figure 7.1 *Of all the servers in all the world, you had to walk into Archie's.*

flames: 'Schofield carn't (sic) write Internet books because she hates Archie' – or some such.

Are you being Servered?

Archie servers can be accessed in two ways: conventionally by telnetting into an Archie server, or by sending search requests to the server by email. The first method is marginally faster than waiting two days or more for an email reply.

To get into an Archie server you telnet to the Archie server of your choice, and a good start is ***archie.doc.ic.ac.uk***. It's at Imperial College in London, and is fairly fast, if you catch it on a good day when it's working and the guy with the beard is back from Majorca. A number of Archie clients are also starting to appear for Windows and Macintosh computers.

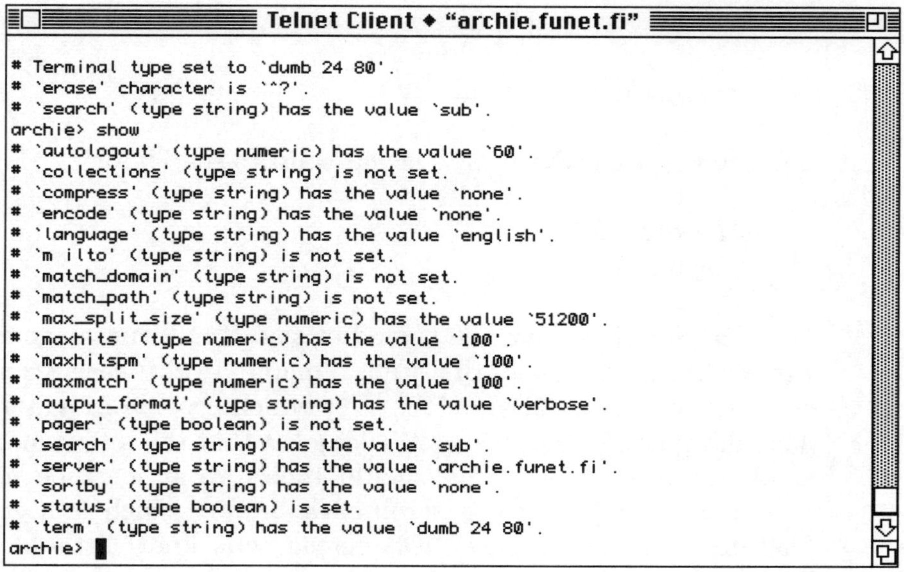

Figure 7.2 *Archie command line settings. Should searching for information be so difficult?*

Search me

Archie uses several search methods to locate the data you want, and all of them are command line driven and come in various guises of complexity. You set up which search method you want after login.

The search methods are:

exact
sub
subcase
regex

You should try the *exact* method first, as long as you know what you're looking for. It's faster, allegedly. However, most people start with *sub*.

You set the search method up with:

set search exact (or *sub* etc.)

and then type in whatever it is you want to search for:

set search sub
prog amiga

The Archie server will then do its stuff and rummage around the world's databases until it finds a match. In this case Archie will come up with a list of all of the sites which provide Amiga files, as a scrolling list. In fact it's such a long list that the information will scroll off your screen. You should therefore at least be using a terminal emulator with a scroll-back buffer, which lets you call back the data for display. DOS people, who know little of scroll-back, will find benefit in a terminal emulation package that logs data to disk. In both cases you'll need to investigate whatever Archie sends you, as you'll get a lot of information back, not all of which will be relevant. But you can use the mail commands to mail the output to yourself.

Archie search methods

The *exact* method looks for an exact match to the search string you've typed in – but there are other choices. Here they are:

Sub matches the search string anywhere in the text. If you typed:

set search sub
prog amigastuff

Archie should find:

amigastuff.lzh
Amigastuff.faq
amigastuff.txt

Subcase matches the search string for case. If you typed:

set search subcase
prog Amiga.stuff

Archie should find:

Amigastuff.faq

It won't find:

amigastuff.txt
amigastuff.lzh

Regex stands for 'regular expression' and is a method of using wildcards to limit search matching. Not many PC or Mac users bother with it, because it's about as intuitive as discovering Relativity. Consequently many personal computer users are happy to do *sub* matching. If you want to get to grips with *regex* searching then you're recommended to pick up a book on UNIX – because typing long search strings hooked together by *regex* expressions leads to more errors than success.

Other Archie commands

You should limit Archie's searching, to provide you with a reasonable number of matches. Archie will look for up to 1000 matches before it gives up, which takes time. You can change this limit with the *maxhits* command:

set maxhits 50

will ensure that you only get the results of 50 matches. A good number is somewhere between 100 and 200.

The *pager* sets up the number of lines displayed on a page, which is normally 24. You can check with the *show* command, and reset the pagination with:

set pager 18 (or some such)

Autologout will set the time allowed before throwing you off. Again, check with *show* before you alter it.

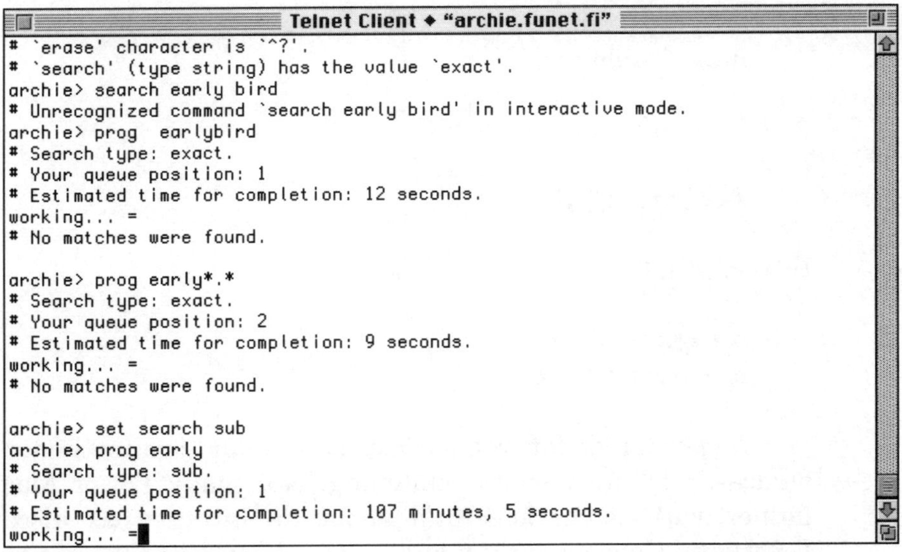

```
Telnet Client ◆ "archie.funet.fi"
# `erase' character is `^?'.
# `search' (type string) has the value `exact'.
archie> search early bird
# Unrecognized command `search early bird' in interactive mode.
archie> prog  earlybird
# Search type: exact.
# Your queue position: 1
# Estimated time for completion: 12 seconds.
working... =
# No matches were found.

archie> prog early*.*
# Search type: exact.
# Your queue position: 2
# Estimated time for completion: 9 seconds.
working... =
# No matches were found.

archie> set search sub
archie> prog early
# Search type: sub.
# Your queue position: 1
# Estimated time for completion: 107 minutes, 5 seconds.
working... =
```

Figure 7.3 *Archie estimates 107 minutes for a search. It's not so good for modem users, unless you use Archie by email.*

Status (on/off) gets Archie to show you the status of the ongoing search, and *sortby* sets the way Archie displays the results. You can set *sortby* to:

hostname/rhostname – which displays the results by alphabetical list of the host on which the search string is found. *Rhostname* gives a reverse alphabetical search.

time/rtime – newest or oldest modification date.

filename/rfilename – alphabetical filename or reverse alphabetical filename.

The availability of commands can vary, so check before you configure Archie to send you nothing, after a long wait.

Archie also has a *whatis* function, which is used instead of the *prog* command. If you type *whatis filename* you might get a list of descriptions of available files. The *whatis* command searches these description lists for matches, and is a slightly more intuitive method of fighting with Archie. But don't forget that Archie doesn't do any file transfers for you – you will still have to FTP to the indicated site and directory to get the data. Progressive it ain't. However, some Archie clients can now do this. They remove all the command line stuff and display the results nicely. You then double click on the file to be FTP'd and it's sent to you directly.

Mailing Archie

You can email search requests to Archie, which makes more sense than hanging around an Archie server consuming telephone time and patience. All the functions mentioned so far will work, and you may find it useful to make up an Archie mail template in your mailer program. You simply send an email to the Archie server of your choice, containing the search requirements, and if you've done everything correctly, you should get a reasonable response. Remember not to send your automatically generated signature to Archie, as it won't appreciate it.

Here's an Archie email request:

Email to archie@archie.doc.ic.ac.uk

---

set mailto sue@s-sco.demon.co.uk
(makes sure you get the response mailed to you)

servers
(returns a list of archie servers)

help
(returns the help file for that server)

set search subcase
pro
Amiga

set maxhits 100

quit
(ends the request.)

And that's it.

If you've done everything properly you should get a reply, usually within a few hours, although it can take longer, like three days, to arrive ... .

Other search methods

Archie is, well, kind of quaint. It's a bit like those stodgy computerized indexes they've now put into municipal libraries. It's quicker to search through the shelves by hand than it is to learn the archaic user interface. There's several more forms of search mechanism on the Internet including Gopher, Veronica and World Wide Web. So if Archie doesn't suit you then look at those other ways of finding what you're after.

Favourite Archie sites

None. But check out the screen shot showing Archie sites.

8 FTP

'FTP works
exceptionally well,
most of the time...'

You're going to like FTP. Everyone does. FTP stands for File Transfer Protocol, and it's the single most popular hobby on the 'Net, if the fact that it takes up 48 per cent of all network traffic is anything to go by. FTP is simply the art of transferring files from one place to another, using the 'file transfer protocol', which gives its name to the process.

FTP comes in two flavours. There's the sort of FTP where you use a terminal emulator and a set of gormless and odd-ball UNIX commands, and the sort of clicky-button FTP which happens on Windows, Macintosh and Amiga machines. In the first case you're back to the character based interface of UNIX, but the newer graphical environments make navigating around remote servers very easy, and you don't have to learn commands such as CD or Grep, or CTRL]. But in both cases you'll need to learn about hierarchical file structures, how to fight with compressed archives, and the mysteries of Anonymous FTP.

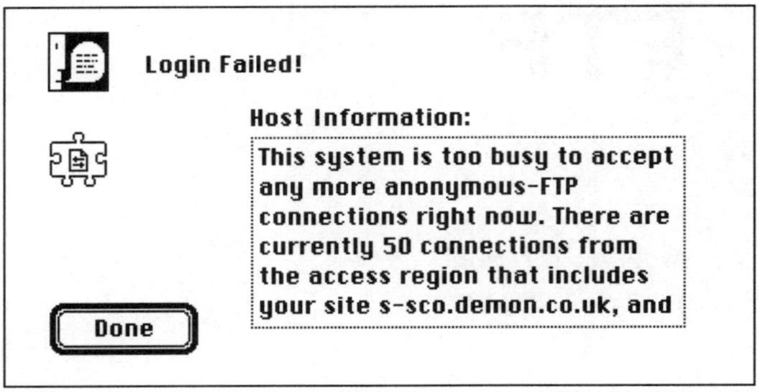

Figure 8.1 *FTP is the single most popular thing on the 'Net. Consequently there might be a few queues.*

Starting up

You'll need an FTP client installed on your machine to use FTP – unless your service provider has got one on his system which you can access via terminal emulation. To get into an FTP site you either type:

ftp sitename

or you fill in an on-screen form containing the information required. Once you get to the log-in screen you'll be asked for a username and password. Here's your first problem. Unless you work at the site, or have bought large amounts of beer for the guy who runs the network, you won't have a login identity. So you use 'anonymous' if you can spell it, and 'ftp' if you can't. Most sites accept either, but for those that don't you'll have to learn to spell, anonymously. For a password you should type your full username and an @ symbol – which makes anonymous FTP rather less anonymous than it would otherwise be. You should then be logged into the system.

However, you'll often find that many FTP sites don't like hordes of people logging in during office hours, or that the number of anonymous users is limited for various reasons. The convention is that anonymous users should keep their FTP usage to a

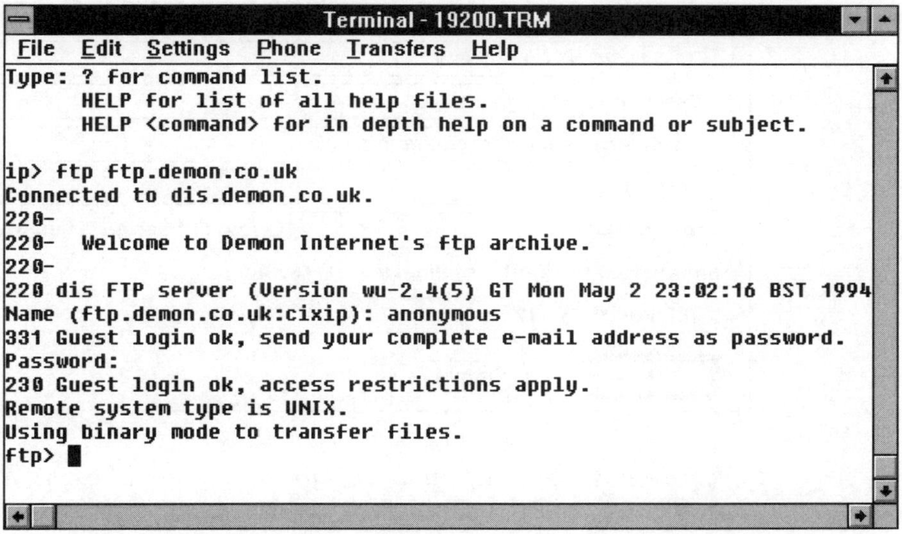

Figure 8.2 *Anonymous login to an ftp server. Use your username as the password.*

minimum during office hours, but that's going to be difficult as it's always office hours somewhere on the Internet. Correspondingly you'll find that many of the more popular ftp sites are constantly busy and you won't be able to get in. But if this is your first ftp experience then try ***ftp.demon.co.uk***. Despite the name you'll still have to type ftp as a command – before typing ftp.demon.co.uk. GUI users will just use ftp.demon.co.uk as the site name.

Once you're in you'll be presented with a directory listing of the files on the server, or at least the files in the first directory of the server. If you're familiar with DOS then you'll know of hierarchical directories, which are a bit like nested Russian dolls. You navigate from the top directory downwards, and have to come back up to the top to go down another branch.

The CD command means change directory, and is used to move around the system. DIR shows the files in the current directory, and GET gets a file. Simple so far? Maybe – but then you have to remember to get your files as either ASCII or binary. ASCII means that you get a plain text file back at the receiving end of things. Binary means you'll receive your file as an executable, or a spreadsheet, or a graphics file – in short as the sort of data your computer doesn't expect you to read with a plain text editor. You

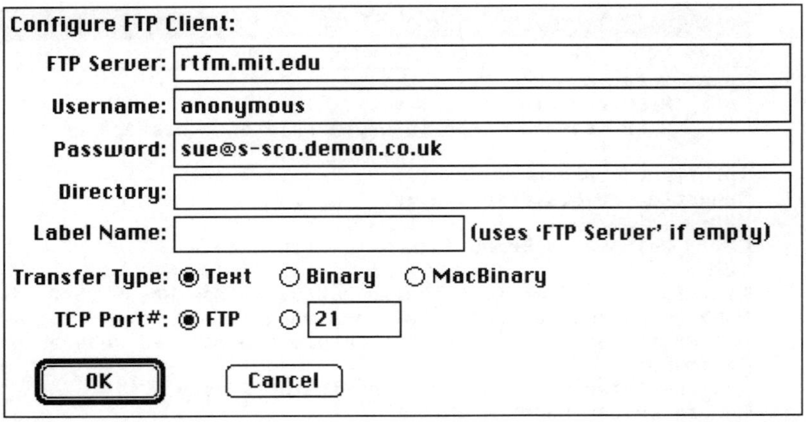

Figure 8.3 *Setting up a GUI for anonymous login. Windows programs need the same parameters.*

tell the remote server which type of transfer you want before you start, by typing in ASCII or binary before the GET command. If you're in any doubt then try binary – except for files which are obviously text files, such as Read Me files, or LS–LR files which contain the directory listings of the server you're on. Binary is sometimes called Image mode – as it sends a binary image of the file on the server, bit by bit. In ASCII mode it just sends the characters of the ASCII alphabet, so what you get on your computer can be read by a text editor. You can get multiple files with the MGET instruction and if you have write access to the remote server you can leave files on it with the PUT command. Most anonymous users will never bother with either of these instructions.

Generally speaking, all of these commands are used only on servers connected to your computer by terminal emulation – you will have a series of button options to navigate and collect files if you're using Windows, Mac or Amiga software. What you may lose with such GUI-based software is the ability to see just how big the remote file is before you start downloading it over a modem link. This can be important, as file transfer speeds over even V32 bis modems can be extremely low due to loading or system usage, and spending half an hour downloading a large file over a modem is quite common. The trick is to look for a file listing the directory details of the ftp server. This will let you see just how big that file is before you try to download it, and directory listings are often kept

Special Offer
Electronic Telegraph Starter Pack

Price list

VAT must be added to all charges

Initial charge	Monthly charge	or	Annual charge
£ ~~25~~	£ 15		£ 180

£15 (normally £25)

Starter Pack
(inc. ET disks, Standard Dial-Up Internet connection, POP3 mail, site and address)

- You may pay by Visa, Access or Mastercard credit cards on a monthly or annual basis.
- You may pay by cheque on an annual basis.
- If taking a Standard Dial-up service paid monthly by credit card, please note that no receipt is issued and you are debited on the first of each month except for the month of joining.
- Companies requiring a VAT receipt must join annually at a cost of £180.00 plus VAT = £211.50.
- Cheques should be made payable to **Demon Internet Ltd.** All payments are due in advance of using any service.
- You are subscribing to **Demon Internet** on an on-going basis. Your account will stay open and you will be invoiced as appropriate until you notify **Demon Internet** in writing that you wish to cancel. You can cancel the Standard Dial-Up service in writing at the end of any month.

This offer is valid until December 31, 1995

Queries
email:etsales@demon.net
Tel: 0181 371 1200
Fax: 0181 371 1201

Application form

First name		Surname		Company name (if applicable)	
tick a box	Mr ☐ Ms ☐	Miss ☐	Mrs ☐	Home telephone number	
Address				Work telephone number	
		Postcode		Date of birth	

Please supply me with the following service/s:

Electronic Telegraph Starter Pack ☐ PC version ☐ Macintosh version

Email address
eg.alan.turner@etgate.co.uk, a.turner@etgate.co.uk or al.turn@etgate.co.uk
__________ @etgate.co.uk

Second choice __________ @etgate.co.uk

Third choice __________ @etgate.co.uk

Method of payment (please tick one box only)

	credit card VISA/MASTERCARD/ACCESS	cheque
monthly	☐	
annually	☐	☐

Credit card number

Expiry date

Signed

Date

Please note: no VAT invoice/receipt issued for monthly accounts

Please send to Electronic Telegraph, Demon Internet Ltd, Gateway House, 322 Regents Park Road, Finchley, London N3 2QQ

Electronic Telegraph
Demon Internet Ltd
Gateway House
322 Regents Park Road
Finchley
London N3 2QQ

in a file called 'Index', or READ.ME or LS LR. To complicate matters those directory listings themselves can be quite large (the one on ftp.demon.co.uk is over two megabytes long) so you'll still have an expensive download just to pick up the directory listing. Other GUI clients have a Get Info button which hops off to the server and grabs the file size and directory information. GUI clients tend not to download this sort of stuff by default, as it takes up even more modem time to get data which you may not be interested in.

What you will also realize when using ftp is that modem connections of any flavour just don't make it as far as economical file transfer is concerned, a theme which will become more apparent as we move on to other Internet based services. But as the only alternative at the moment is an ISDN or leased line we must wait for the Information Superhighway to become a reality, say in ten or twelve years' time. In the meantime you can buy CD-ROMs containing many of the more popular Internet ftp archives. There's SIMTEL for DOS, CICA archives for Windows – and any number of Info-Mac clones for the Mac. These cost between £12 and £50 in the UK, less in the USA, and are, at the moment, the most cost-effective methods of distributing software normally found on the Internet. You can order them by email from the USA. Mail Joe@config.sys for a list.

FTP arcanery

If you're using a terminal to hook into ftp you'll see that each command you type in to the server results in some sort of output, preceded by a three-number digit. This is put there, not so that the guy with the beard and sandals who is looking after the remote site can suss out these diagnostic codes, but so your ftp program can take appropriate action if there's an error. Most ftp programs don't bother with these numbers, because if they did, writers would have to fill up needless pages in books with long and sordid explanations of what they mean.

And what about those codes you see before a file, like -rw- -rw-r- -? These are the attribute settings for the file or directory, and are called 'permission masks'. You only need to know that if you need to know more you should be buying UNIX books, and that 'r' stands for 'read only'. You shouldn't be able to overwrite a read-

```
ls-lR
total 1080
drwxrwsr-x  4 root          512 Mar  4 23:23 4.3
drwxrwsr-x  2 peter         512 Mar  4 23:18 BSD
-rw-rw-r--  1 root         3398 Apr 21 15:24 FTPVIEW.TXT
drwxrwsr-x  2 root          512 Mar  4 22:14 NeXT
drwxrwsr-x  7 root          512 Mar  4 23:23 SCO
drwxr-sr-x  3 root          512 Apr  7 16:40 VAX
lrwxrwxrwx  1 root            8 Mar  4 23:38 accu -> /pub/cug
drwxrwsr-x 21 oliver       1024 May 11 20:35 amiga
drwxrwsr-x 15 ubik          512 Apr  6 01:05 antivirus
drwxrwsr-x  4 arcturus     1024 May 11 06:15 archimedes
drwxrwsr-x  7 root          512 Apr  7 16:54 archives
drwxrwsr-x  5 chaos         512 Apr 16 23:52 atari
drwxrwsr-x  5 peter         512 May  6 11:49 books
drwxrwsr-x  2 root          512 Mar  4 23:24 commercial-demos
drwxrwsr-x  2 root         1024 May  1 18:04 cpm
drwxrwsr-x 12 root          512 May  8 14:46 cug
```

Figure 8.4 *Permission masks on an FTP server.*

only file or change its name or do any of those things which, in the UK, will put you in breach of the Computer Misuse Act. And you won't see those masks under many of the GUI based programs, which is yet another blessing, although a Show File Information or Get Info button should bring them up.

Here are some useful terminal commands for ftp:

cd fred	– changes to directory 'fred'
cdup	– goes up one directory
cd /	– go to top of tree
cd ..	– go up one subdirectory
asc	– sets file transfers to ASCII
bin	– sets file transfer as binary
mget	– use for multiple file receives (not with GUIs)
cd / nextdir	– changes to a new directory.

Don't forget to leave a space between the / and everything else as you need a space after the first word. And don't forget that these commands may differ from server to server. And ... UNIX file and directory names are case sensitive. FREd is different from FReD, just to make life as difficult as possible.

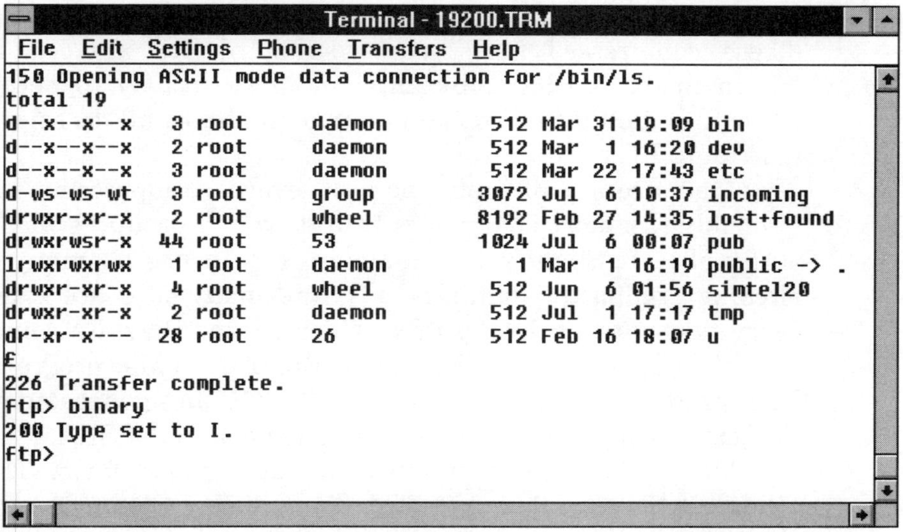

Figure 8.5 *Set binary mode before downloading executables or compressed files. 'Type set to I' means Image mode, that is, binary.*

File compression

Users of bulletin boards, dial-up services and the Internet will be well aware that most computer files can be compressed down into around a half of their original size or less, by the use of file compression programs such as PKZip, Stuffit, Compact Pro and the like.

There are many reasons for compressing files, the most obvious being the need to fit more files in a given area – be that a local hard disk or a network server. File compression utilities are also useful for adding two or more files into a single bundle for transmission over modems or for adding encryption or password protection to files. Some compression programs also allow compressed files to be filed to disk in segments for reconstitution at a later date (multi-disk segmenting). And most compression programs also have an option to create self-extracting archives. These let users decompress files without access to the original program (but can add about ten per cent or more to the size of the compressed archive.)

The most common format for compressed PC files is PKZip. These compressed files have a suffix of ZIP and you'll need PKUnzip (or a PKUnzip-compliant clone utility) to decompress these files. You'll find such an animal on almost all ftp servers that distribute PC files.

Mac users will come across several compression utilities. Probably the most common is Stuffit, which produces files with a suffix of SIT. Slightly less common, but in use on many dial-up sites, is Compactor (suffix is cpt), and many sites are starting to carry files with an LZH suffix, which means they are compressed with the Mac version of LHA, titled MacLHA. A Mac program called Zipit produces some compatibility with ZIP files generated on PCs. Self-extracting Mac Archives often have a suffix of SEA.

Many Mac sites carry files in 'disk image' form. This is a scheme where a bit image of a floppy disk is compressed into a single file, and the corresponding decompressor is used to re-create the disk image. This process either creates a floppy disk with the original information on it, or mounts an image of the virtual floppy onto the desktop. DiskCopy is the utility to do the former, MountImage to do the latter and disk image files often carry the suffix 'image'. MountImage is sometimes the more useful of the two, as it allows users of pre-SuperDrive Macs to mount an image of a 1.44 megabyte disk on the desktop of a Mac which can only read 800 kB floppies. You'll find image files used to carry copies of Apple installer disks, for instance.

Let's go one step further and consider what happens to files when you load them up to the Internet. As mentioned previously, your file has to be translated to coexist with the antiquated file structure of the Internet, and a utility called BinHex effects this transmutation on Macs, and UUencode does the same on PCs. BinHex or UUencode translates your neat and tidy binary file into an ASCII representation of its hex code. This can then be squirted around the Internet with impunity as a text file and restored to binary on reception. (BinHex files have a .HQX suffix.) FTP handles PC binary files as bit images, so they come and go as binary files, but you will have to tell your FTP client that you want a binary transfer in almost every case. It's a common mistake to download binary files as ASCII, in which case they don't work when you get them.

As if that wasn't enough, the UNIX fraternity often decide

that an additional compression process is needed to compress compressed files while they live on the server, and many Internet servers now use a GNU-ZIP variant to do this. The result is that you'll need yet another process to unlock your data. These files have a gz suffix and you'll need Gzip to turn the file into binary, Binhex or UUencode format. Some sites purport to do this for you automatically if you put a + sign before your password, and Imperial College, London runs just such a scheme. But despite some correspondence between the author and the comms guru at src.doc.ic.ac.uk this scheme wouldn't work for this writer and a number of other correspondents.

There are a number of other compression schemes around. LHA is used on both Amiga and PC files, and is creeping across to the Mac platform, and ZOO files are starting to catch on, although the older ARC utility is slowly fading away. You can find decompression utilities for all of these files in a number of places, so getting hold of them should not be a problem.

Graphics stuff

Graphics files are stored on ftp servers in various formats, the most common being GIF files, the most uncommon being Mac 'picts'. Other formats abound, and you'll generally need the right sort of file viewer on your computer to view and manipulate graphics files. GIF files will go straight into most graphics programs on most types of computer, and GIF files are consequently the lingua franca of ftp and dial-up comms users. TIFF files, on the other hand, come in a dozen different types and are not guaranteed to cross computer boundaries smoothly. There are also JPEG files, and TGA files (targa). TARGA files are slowly being replaced by JPEG files. As mentioned, you'll need a graphics viewer of some sort to see these files on your PC or Mac (the Amiga comes with one built in, of course). Graphics Workshop is a good all-rounder for the PC, and Graphics Convertor is arguably the best all-round Shareware graphics program for the Mac, or any other platform. Both are readily available on the Internet from many ftp sites.

Graphics file transfers

Once you've grabbed the file from an FTP server you may want to share it around a little. Your friends will all have their own ideas about what constitutes a computer so you'll need to learn ways of sharing graphics files around. The trick is to bring the file into a common disk format, and then convert it into a common file format. Mac, Amiga and Atari machines have utilities that let them save files in MS-DOS formats – but if all else fails (and you have a modem) you can upload the file from the alien computer to your favourite email service, and then download it to your computer for conversion. Other tricks include using null modem cables between serial ports.

Most of the Mac's graphics translator programs will work with most graphics files on MS-DOS disks – for instance, if you have a Windows BMP file on a PC floppy disk then Apple File Exchange will read it into the Mac without error. It can then be translated with Graphic Convertor or similar. But Mac users often run into problems with TIFF and EPS files. TIFF files have many inherent formatting differences, including black and white, grey scale, 24-bit, 4-bit and 8-bit images. TIFF also supports the use of multiple types of data compression – and to complicate matters further, two byte-ordering schemes are supported (Intel and Motorola), as indicated by the internal TIFF file header. So don't be surprised if you have problems loading ftp'd TIFFs into your computer.

PC based Encapsulated PostScript Files on the PC come as either plain ASCII files, or binary files with a header that describes both the PostScript commands and the preview (TIFF or Metafile) section of the file. Again, not all EPS files will translate between computers or platforms, so if you have a choice, go for GIF.

Getting the best from FTP

FTP works exceptionally well, most of the time. It runs slowly if the remote server is busy or the route your TCP/IP packets take is busy, or if you don't have the correct form of 'handshaking' on the modem link. You can multitask FTP sessions if you have the right

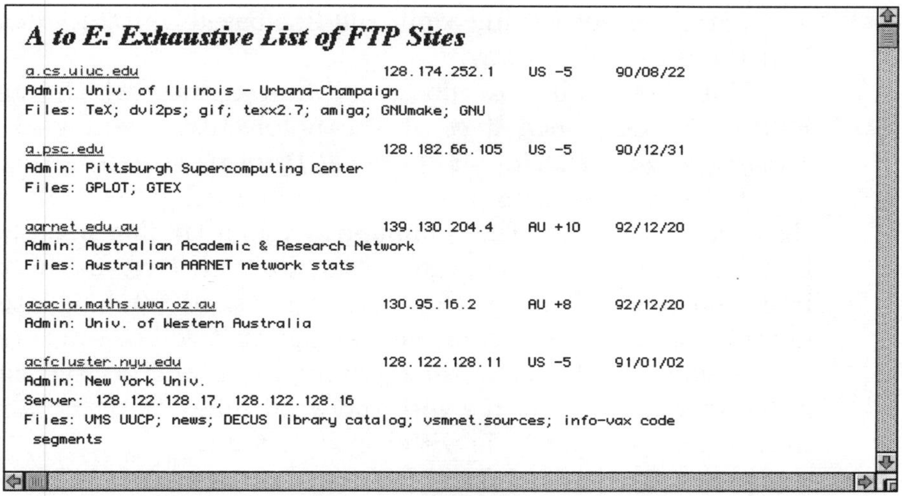

A to E: Exhaustive List of FTP Sites

```
a.cs.uiuc.edu                      128.174.252.1    US -5     90/08/22
Admin: Univ. of Illinois - Urbana-Champaign
Files: TeX; dvi2ps; gif; texx2.7; amiga; GNUmake; GNU

a.psc.edu                          128.182.66.105   US -5     90/12/31
Admin: Pittsburgh Supercomputing Center
Files: GPLOT; GTEX

aarnet.edu.au                      139.130.204.4    AU +10    92/12/20
Admin: Australian Academic & Research Network
Files: Australian AARNET network stats

acacia.maths.uwa.oz.au             130.95.16.2      AU +8     92/12/20
Admin: Univ. of Western Australia

acfcluster.nyu.edu                 128.122.128.11   US -5     91/01/02
Admin: New York Univ.
Server: 128.122.128.17, 128.122.128.16
Files: VMS UUCP; news; DECUS library catalog; vsmnet.sources; info-vax code
 segments
```

Figure 8.6 *More FTP sites than you can shake a modem at. Use World Wide Web to find them.*

sort of client software – that is, you can log into two or more sites and download files concurrently, which is a good way of economizing on modem use. But if you open too many sessions you'll slow things down considerably.

One tip (for V32 bis and faster modems) is to watch the RD (receive data) light on your modem. If it's not continuously lit then your modem isn't constantly occupied. Try opening another FTP session and starting a second download. You may find that you can take advantage of spare bandwidth on your dial-up link. Alas, if your computer has an internal modem you won't have any lights to look at but you might have an on-screen indicator which shows how much data is arriving in a given time. Other tips for achieving low-cost transfers include using FTP at 3 a.m. – Eastern Standard Time, and buying CD-ROMs with the files already on them.

FTP by mail

With commendable foresight, and the magic of the word processor, Chapter 4 mentioned that you could get files by email from any site so equipped to do that. FTPMAIL will test your patience to the full as it entails programming command-line based UNIX systems from four thousand miles away.

The first thing to do is to find a site which supports FTPMAIL. One such lives at the notoriously overloaded ***mail-server@rtfm.mit.edu***, another is at ***ftpmail.sunsite.unc.edu***.

Both of these sites provide an ftp-by-mail gateway to most of the other ftp servers. The command syntax is similar on both. Start by sending an email message to the site with Help in the subject line, and in the body of the text. Don't send your signature, or anything else in the body of the message or it will be interpreted as a command. At the same time you might as well get the top-level index so add a second line with the word Index on it and finish off in true code-warrior style with the word Quit:

help
index
quit

Then wait for the result. On Boxing Day 1994, mail went full circle in about 20 minutes. In the middle of a US semester it might take a lot longer. The help file you'll get will look like the following, which is a truncated version:

From: File Transfer by Mail <ftpmail@sunsite.unc.edu>
Date: Mon, 26 Dec 1994 07:38:01 -0500
To: sue@s-sco.demon.co.uk
Subject: <FTP EMAIL> response

<FTP EMAIL> response
ftpmail@sunsite.unc.edu – ftp's files and sends them back via electronic mail.

If you have problems please email ftpkeeper@sunsite.unc.edu and quote the following line:
$Revision: 1.23 $

Valid commands to the ftpmail gateway are:

reply-to email-address
Who to send the response to. This is optional and defaults to the users email address –

followed by one of:

help	*Just send back help*
delete jobid	*Delete the given job*
open [site [user [pass]]]	*Site to ftp to.* *Defaults are sunsite.unc.edu anonymous reply-to-address.*

If there was an open then it can be followed by up to 100 of the following commands:

cd pathname	*Change directory.*
ls [pathname]	*Short listing of pathname. Default pathname is current directory.*
dir [pathname]	*Long listing of pathname. Default pathname is current directory.*
get pathname	*Get a file and email it back.*
compress	*Compress files/dir-listings before emailing back*
gzip	*Gzip files/dir-listings before emailing back*
mode binary	
mode ascii	*Change the mode selected for the get command. Defaults to binary.*
quit	*End of input – ignore any following lines.*

Example scripts are:

open
dir
quit

(Connect to sunsite.unc.edu and send back the contents of the top level directory)

reply-to lmjm@doc.ic.ac.uk
open
cd unix
get buffer.shar
quit

(Connect to sunsite.unc.edu and send back the file buffer.shar to lmjm@doc.ic.ac.uk)

open src.doc.ic.ac.uk
cd graphics/X11/X.V11R5
get ls-lR.Z
cd ../contrib
compress
ls -ltra
quit

(Connect to src.doc.ic.ac.uk, send back the file ls-lR.Z in graphics/X11/X.V11R5. As this is a binary file it has to be transferred in binary mode. Because it is binary it will automatically be uuencoded (the default binary encoder). Then change to ../contrib and mail back a compressed directory listing. Although compressing ls output makes it binary, which then has to be encoded, it still ends up smaller than the original.)

As you'll see from the examples it's possible to use FTPMAIL effectively, as long as you're prepared to learn the scripting. However it's a far cry from using a graphical FTP client on a direct TCP/IP connection, although as you'll agree, it's much better than nothing.

Favourite FTP sites

FTP sites are too numerous to list, but a good way to get to them is with Gopher or World Wide Web. That way you can find a site which carries the information you need. Rather than list more than a handful of sites it's suggested you read the Gopher chapter and start from there. Here are a few sites to whet your appetite.

ftp.demon.co.uk is a good UK site. It carries almost all of the software you need to get going, plus lists of FAQs (Frequently Asked Questions) and lists of other lists.

mrcnext.cso.uiuc.edu has the Project Gutenberg files. Project

Gutenberg was set up to carry non-copyright works of literature in electronic form, and has much of interest.

toybox.gsfc.nasa.gov carries space images, but the site can be slow during the rush hour. Modem users beware.

wiretap.spies.com carries electronic books, stuff on privacy issues and much electronic bric-a-brac, and is almost always available.

ftp.uu.net

Internet Talk Radio in

> /usenet/news.answers/internet-talk-radio/anonymous-ftp-list.Z.

These are monster (20–30 Mbyte) files containing the Internet Talk Radio files, a sort of Radio Internet. Features include 'Geek of the Week'.

titan.ksc.nasa.gov for the WinVN NNTP Newsreader.

sseop.jsc.nasa.gov for yet more shuttle images.

ames.arc.nasa.gov in pub/GIF for yet more space images, ds.internic.net for InterNIC Directory of directories.

csd4.csd.uwm.edu for inet.services.txt (Yanoff's Services List).

nic.merit.edu (documents/fyi/ and documents/rfc) – For Your Information and Requests For Comments files.

gorgon.tft.tele.no – Yellow Pages in pub/groupware. But the USA version, not the UK one.

gopher.netsys.com on port 2100 for Electronic News4Stand.

merlot.welch.jhu.edu – biology info.

gopher.msen.com – jobs in US.

marvel.loc.gov – Library of Congress Machine Assisted Realization of the Virtual Electronic Library.

fatty.law.cornell.edu – Cornell Law School Information.

9 Gopher

'You could get to
like gopher-ing with
Veronica...'

Gopher is either a dreadful misuse of the English language ('go fer it') or a burrowing rodent of the family Geomyidae. And if we are being tautological in a zoological sense we might quibble that Gopherus, the burrowing tortoise of North America, bears more resemblance to the electronic variety than Geomyidae, as neither is particularly fast when it comes to modems. So Gopher is an information search tool, which originally came from the University of Minnesota, which has a Gopher of the Geomyidae variety as a mascot. You use Gopher to search for things on the 'Net – but unlike Archie, Gopher is menu driven. You could get to like Gophering, whereas the same cannot always be said for Archie-ing.

To set about Gophering you need a Gopher client on your computer at best – or the use of a telnet client over a terminal link at worst. You open your Gopher client (you have already connected to the 'Net by modem or Ethernet) and start clicking on menus, or fighting with typed-in commands. Gopher is client-dependent –

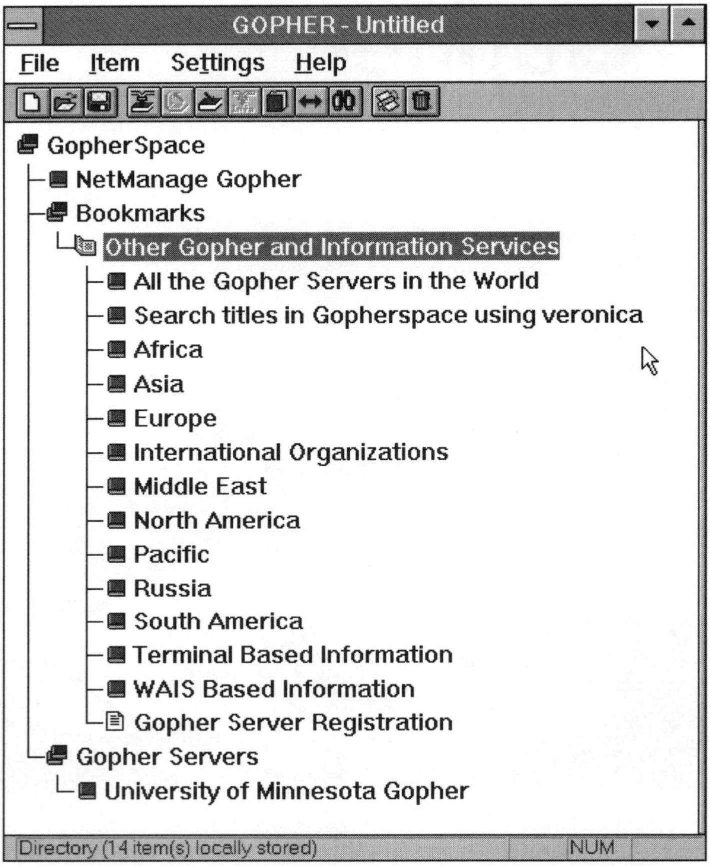

Figure 9.1 *This is the Gopher client from Internet Chameleon. Navigation is by point and click.*

that is, some Gopher clients are pretty poor, some are just pretty, and some are just poor. Windows users get a good Gopher client in Internet Chameleon, and in the Shareware HGopher software. Mac users will love TurboGopher, which is also Shareware and as fast as they come.

The speed of the Gopher client you are using is fairly important, especially so over phone lines where you're paying money not to receive data. And Gopher likes to pull pictures off the 'Net and show them to you, so a speedy user interface is vital. You can get most of the latest releases of Gopher software from the ftp site at ***boombox.micro.umn.edu*** but alas the site is often busy.

Most service providers can also get you the software so ask there if in doubt.

I know I want it – but what does it do?

Gopher pulls information off the 'Net. It's a 'document delivery service' which can get you text files, binaries, images, executable and plain old lists. Gopher was originally developed in April 1991 by the University of Minnesota and consequently you'll find that many Gopher clients default to the University of Minnesota on start-up.

Gopher in actuality is a bunch of dedicated computers called Gopher servers. Each Gopher server knows about all the other servers (most of the time), so if a Gopher server doesn't have the info you want it should go and look it up elsewhere at another Gopher server. It presents these searches as a series of menus from which you pick the next item you want. You navigate around between Gopher servers, or you search either a particular server for information, or all of the servers, or just all the menu titles on all the servers (menu titles contain preset pointers to major services like Electronic Books). The All Servers approach means that you have discovered GopherSpace – that hypothetical realm inhabited by those stupid boxes of silicon we are pleased to call computers.

Using GopherSpace

You can access a Gopher server either by using the Gopher client stored on the computer at your Internet provider's end, or more commonly by using your very own Gopher client software. You can also telnet into a Gopher server and do it that way, but running your own client software is faster, and you get a say in what the interface looks like. Most Gopher client software comes ready configured with a 'home' server. This is usually the University of Minnesota, as previously mentioned.

If you've got your client software from an Internet provider then the home page might reflect his interest in selling you connect time, but generally speaking, the University of Minnesota is where Gopher tyros end up. Once you're connected you will be presented

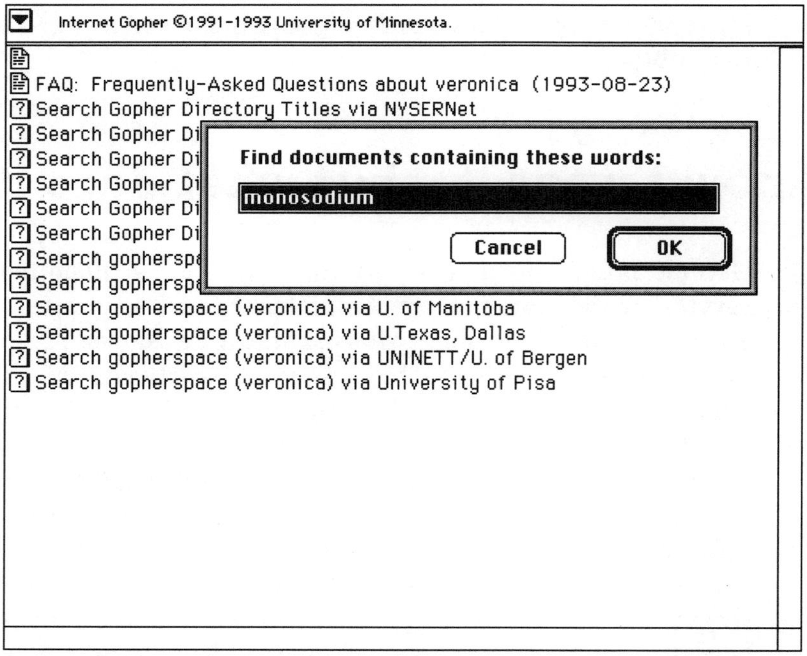

Figure 9.2 *Gopher searches GopherSpace (other Gopher servers). Veronica lets you search multiple sites for keywords.*

with a menu of places to go, things to do, and it's up to you to start exploring. You do this by actioning menu requests and following menu items until you get to where you want to be. This is easier than it sounds but in the early days of your Gophering you will neither know where you want to go, nor recognize where you are once you get there. But it doesn't take long to navigate around the system, and after a while you'll really get the feeling that GopherSpace is a rather good term for the virtual environment you're in whilst Gophering.

Veronica

After a couple of hours of floating around in GopherSpace you are going to ask how to find specific items in such a sea of menus? The answer is the 'Very Easy Rodent-Oriented Net-wide Index to Computerized Archives', or Veronica. Of course it is.

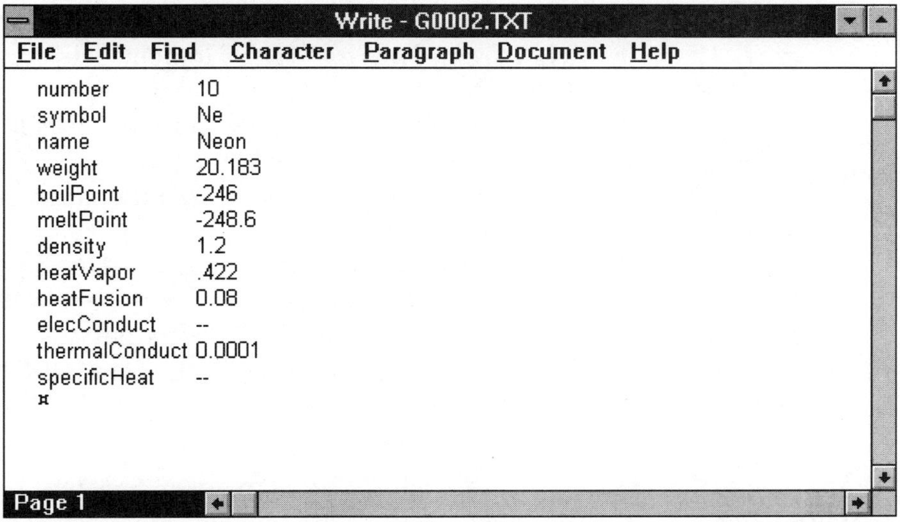

Figure 9.3 *If you use a GUI Gopher client, it will hook into other programs to display the result. Text files from Gopher can be automatically displayed in Windows Write, for instance.*

You get to Veronica by following Gopher menus to ***Search topics in GopherSpace using Veronica***. You'll get to a further set of menus from where you choose a Gopher server (pick the one nearest to you). Picking one site then lets you type in a search string, and off it goes to get the data. You'll get a response in seconds, or more probably you'll get a message saying that the Gopher you chose as a gateway for searching is too busy to handle your request. You can either try again, or go to another server. If you search 'Gopher directory titles' you'll just be searching the menus available on the Gopher servers, which is useful for those common searches like Lists of Gopher Servers (search on Lists). If you search 'GopherSpace' you'll be looking at all of the indexes, and you'll find many more files that match your search criteria.

If you know where the information you want is you can usually go straight to that server and type in your request. This saves network bandwidth and should speed things up a tad, although many Gopher servers seem to be permanently busy these days. In both cases you'll be rewarded with screens full of information which matches the keyword typed in, and your heart will surge with joy. Or you'll be cross and bitter because the server is busy or it cannot find what you want and then your heart will be dour and grey. It's worthwhile remembering that Gopher gets about the Internet by telnet and that if you do find a site you're interested in and want to return to you can telnet there yourself. But it's often quicker to Gopher around, especially if you have a GUI Gopher client, because you don't have to muck around with UNIX's demands for login codes and so forth.

You may also run into the phenomenon of The De-Clienting of GopherSpace – where network administrators remove telnet clients from their Gopher servers on the basis that it's better if you use your own. This is also a great move towards the Coming GUI-ness of GopherSpace and the day may come when you'll never see a command line interface ever again.

Bookmarks

Once you discover bookmarks you'll wonder why the Internet is reputed to be so difficult. The Gopher client lets you navigate back to places you've already been by way of bookmarks. You find a Gopher server which contains, say, the entire text of 'The Big Dummy's Guide to the Hitch-Hikers Guide to the Art of Derivative Book Titles', and you want to go back there when Kevin arrives with the brown ale and the modem. You set a Gopher bookmark (methods vary depending on the access method) which will take you back to the site or archive you were at when you set it. On a Mac or a PC those bookmarks will still be there the next time you use your Gopher client – but alas, if you telnet to a Gopher site you'll lose your bookmarks as soon as you disconnect. But at least it's a great way of justifying an upgrade to a Mac or Windows computer.

Getting files with Gopher

Gopher is user friendly, despite that fact that the server side of things runs under UNIX. The latest Mac and Windows versions of the client software (using something called HGopher) can do as many things at once as you've got the memory for, which rather makes you wonder how DOS ever got to be so popular. You can kick off a search in one window, navigate in another, and download a file

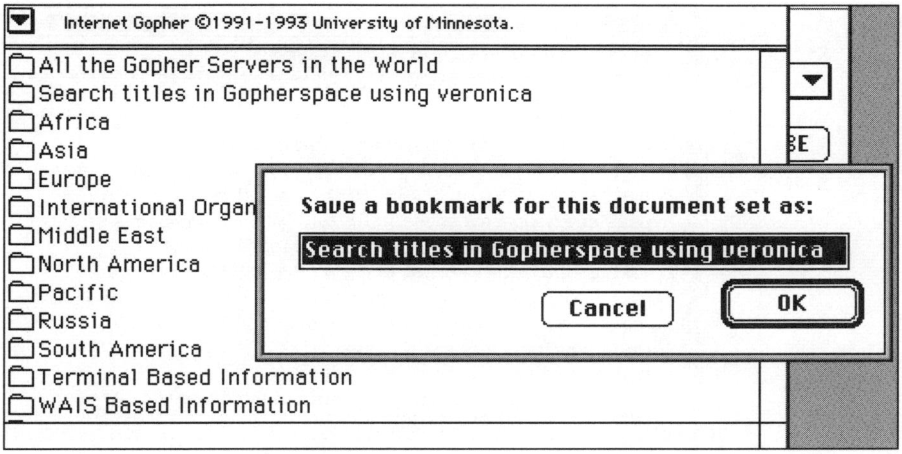

Figure 9.4 *Bookmarks let you save navigation points or pointers to entire documents in your client software. If you use bookmarks on a terminal service you'll lose them when you log off.*

in a third – as long as your modem, your service provider and your personal computer can take the strain. Gopher can then download the file to you via FTP or, if you're using a terminal, via one of the asynchronous file transfer protocols like Zmodem or Xmodem.

GUI Gopher software can also be hooked into other programs you've got sitting on your computer, and will display GIF files online if it can find a GIF viewer, or pick up and play sound files if you have the matching software and hardware installed. In fact Gopher is the single most really neat way of finding files and data on the 'Net, and one can only wonder why it's such a comparatively recent introduction. If you're confused about why you should be using Gopher servers instead of Archie to locate files and data – remember that Archie provides pointers to FTP sites, while Gopher is an archive indexing system in its own right. In many cases you'll be able to find what you need with Gopher – but in some cases you still need Archie. And the astute Internetter will use both methods to find files, and perhaps use Gopher for a bit of recreation.

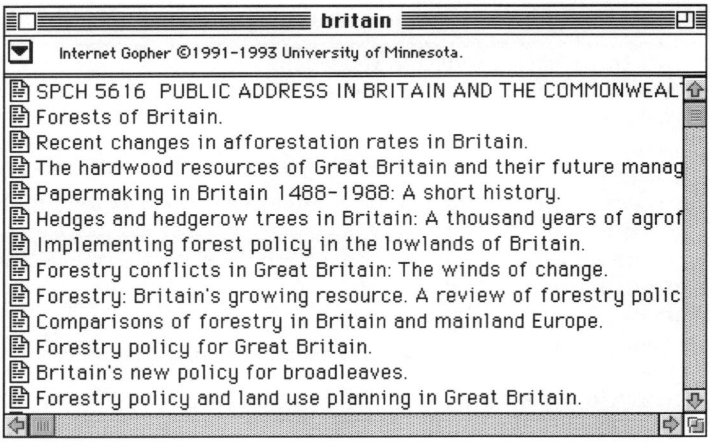

Figure 9.5 *Any of these documents can be pulled down as files to your hard disk. Gopher also knows about FTP so you can get executables via Gopher, too.*

WAIS

WAIS is Wide Area Information Server, and it normally gets a chapter to itself in yer average Internet book. It doesn't get one here because the WAIS servers themselves are in a constant state of being rehashed – which means that any examples given may not work – and you may find that you can get all the information you need from the Internet using Gopher. (Gopher can pick up WAIS servers as part of its ferreting.)

The main advantage of WAIS over Gopher is that it will search multiple WAIS servers at one swoop, whereas Gopher takes a peek inside one at a time. WAIS servers also tend to carry a lot of academic files, and it's consequently of great use for scientific or academic research.

You get to a WAIS server by telnetting to one, or by using the WAIS client you almost certainly don't have on your machine. Or you can get to WAIS via the World Wide Web, which is getting to be the grandaddy of all Internet search mechanisms. Try telnetting to quake.think.com as your first attempt – it was running as this book went to press. Type WAIS at the login prompt, to get to the WAIS front end.

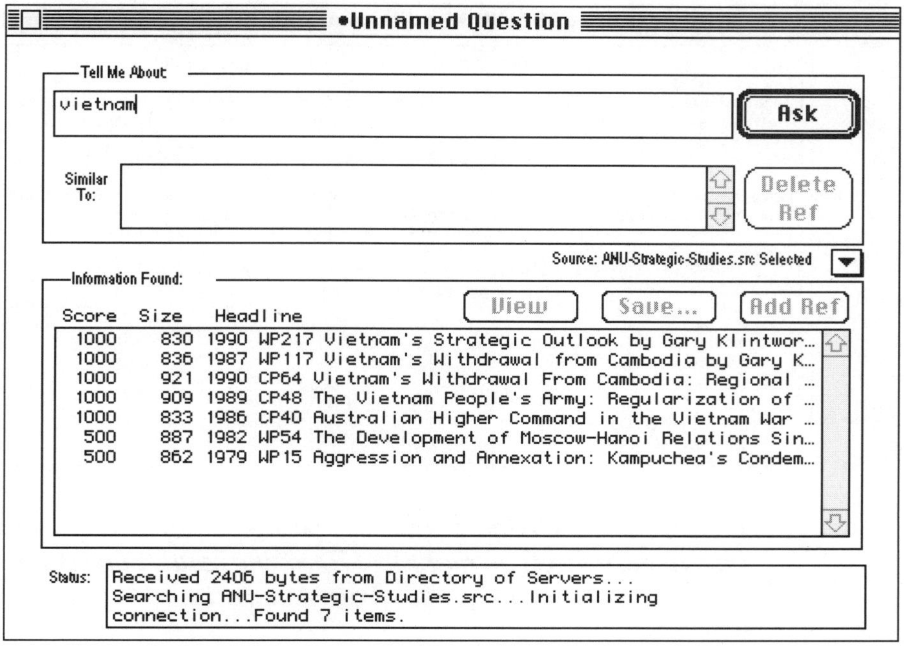

Figure 9.6 *Searching WAIS servers can be quick – but you can get them with both Gopher and World Wide Web. You don't need a dedicated WAIS client to get involved.*

WAIS servers used to present the user with a list of other WAIS servers but had to stop when the list started to edge up to several hundred sites. So WAIS (at quake.think.com) now presents only the top directory, which might not mean much if you've not WAISed before.

You search through WAIS-space by entering a keyword – you'll be given a prompt – and then picking from a list of databases which contain the keyword you entered. With some WAIS clients you can point the search at a single server or the whole list of WAIS servers, which will provide more results, quantitatively speaking.

Telnet WAIS screens are a bit picky about the sort of terminal emulation you have – you need to be able to select an item from the list by moving up and down, which means your terminal emulation has to work well. If it doesn't work like that then try typing in the number in brackets you'll see at the end of each search item.

The Boolean search mechanism is simple – if you want to refine the search you can use AND, OR, NOT as separators – but

Figure 9.7 *WAIS tends to point to available academic resources, as well as real files. Here, the result of a search points towards a record available from Australia.*

not all WAIS servers will work with them.

As an example, if you want to search on 'arabic' and 'grammar' you enter the two keywords separated by a space:

arabic AND grammar

(Don't use 'and' in lower case.) You'll get a list of search results back, with the number of 'hits' per search (out of 1000) indicated in the Score Column. Pick up the document with the space bar and if it's what you want you can mail it to yourself by hitting the M key, or by following the prompt.

If you find WAIS useful then try the Gopher method of accessing it, which might be quicker. And if you get really hooked on WAIS then you can get WAIS client software for your machine from several sites, notably by FTPing to wais.com and looking in /pub/freeware. Some of the WAIS clients are much easier to use than the character based interface you get with telnet, and the MacWAIS client in particular is a joy to behold. As always, the client software varies in its usability, so if you have a choice, shop around.

Which one when?

It's crunch time. You've worked through this book, and come across several methods for locating files on the Internet. Which one should you use?

Despite protestations from Internet geeks armed with Ethernet terminals and UNIX, the best method of searching the Internet is the one you're happiest with. Archie is slow and command line based – which means you can use it from almost any dial-up provider via a terminal connection; WAIS works best with a GUI client and provides a direct link to many academic databases. But Gopher is the easiest of the lot, and the fastest over modem links. It can also hook into those WAIS servers, and so it perhaps offers the best compromise. It's worth spending a little time exploring Gopher client programs too, as they differ in their ability to present information in a coherent manner. And you may have to configure your Gopher client to bring up various file viewers; as an example the Windows Gopher programs tend to bring up 'Write' for text files, Paintbrush for BMP files and so on. You'll need to spend some time fine-tuning this aspect of your Gophering to get the best from it.

Finally, Gophering is one of the nicest ways of giving money to your telecomms provider – it provides a key to many of the doors on the Internet. Go for Gopher.

Clever Gopher stuff (1)

Gopher provides labels which tell you what sort of file you're looking at. You won't see these 'file identifiers' if you're using a graphic Gopher client (which will show them as icons) but you will see them with a character based client:

0 Item is a file.
1 Item is a directory.
2 Item is a CSO (qi) phone-book server.
3 Error.
4 Item is a BinHexed Macintosh file.
5 Item is a DOS binary archive of some sort.

6 Item is a UNIX UUencoded file.
7 Item is an Index-Search server.
8 Item points to a text-based telnet session.
9 Item is a binary file! Your client must read it fully (until the connection closes). This could take a while on a large file.

T TN3270 connection.

Experimental IDs:

s Sound type.
g GIF type.
M MIME type. Item contains MIME data.
h html type.
I Image type.
i 'inline' text type.

Clever Gopher stuff (2) – enhanced Veronica searching

When you select a query type, your Gopher client will present a dialog box. The search is not case-sensitive.

You may get better results by entering a multi-word query rather than a single word. Multi-word queries will find only those items whose titles contain all of the specified words. For instance, 'book' might find 4000 items, but 'Apple PowerBook' will find 2000.

By default, the Veronica servers will deliver only the first 200 items that match your query. You can request any number of items by including the '-mx' command phrase in your query. X is the number of items you wish.

'book -m' will provide all available matching items.

'book -m1000' will provide 1000 items.

You may find a message at the end of your Veronica results menu:

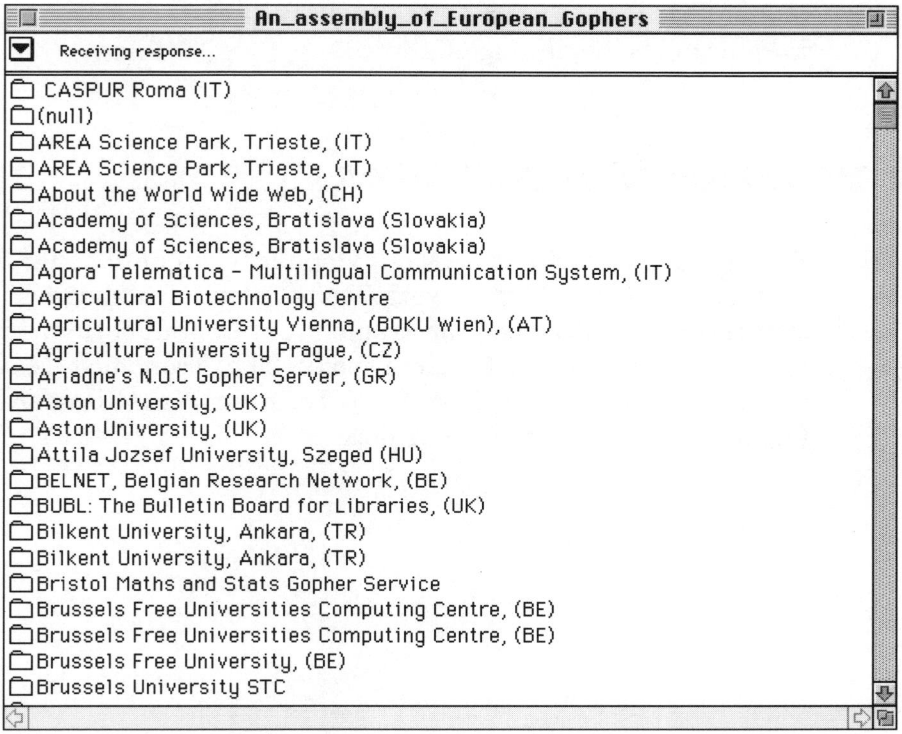

Figure 9.8 *A warren of EuroGophers. Pick servers outside the USA for faster searches.*

"*** There are 59173 more items matching your query ****"

Use ' book -m' to rerun the search and get all the items.

Boolean Veronica searches

The search understands the logical operators AND, NOT, OR.

If you use a simple multi-word query, such as 'mammal whale', it is the same as using AND between the words. For instance 'book electronic' is the same query as 'electronic and book'. An asterisk ('*') at the end of a query will match anything, so use it as a limited form of wildcard search. The asterisk character may be used only at the end of words as the search will fail if a '*' is placed within a word or at the beginning of a word.

Favourite Gopher sites

They're all wonderful. Check out Gopher menu options for 'all the Gopher servers in the world' and start rummaging. Some interesting places are the Electronic Frontier Foundation, set up by Lotus 1-2-3 salesman Mitch Kapoor, The Economist Magazine, Islamic resources, Schoolnet, Long Term Ecological Research, and Papyrus. After that, take your pick.

10 World Wide Web

'Necessity is the
smotherer of convention'
Lambert Jeffries

Sit back a minute, and think about personal computers. You might dwell on just how poorly designed they are, or why this year's model always costs a thousand pounds but has a second-hand value of three hundred, or why, after the tens of billions of dollars spent on research, we still don't have a decent user interface. Then congratulate yourself. You've turned into a computer visionary, and if you should put your thoughts to word processor, you will certainly become a millionaire.

Computer visionaries were around long before personal computers were invented. Babbage was one, Clive Sinclair another. Some of the later visionaries even had the benefit of technology. They put their thoughts into deeds and invented graphical user interfaces, Internet Relay Chat, Doom and Visicalc, in no particular order. Others invented concepts which seemed odd at the time, but now are starting to bring real benefits to computer users as the technology to make them feasible becomes available.

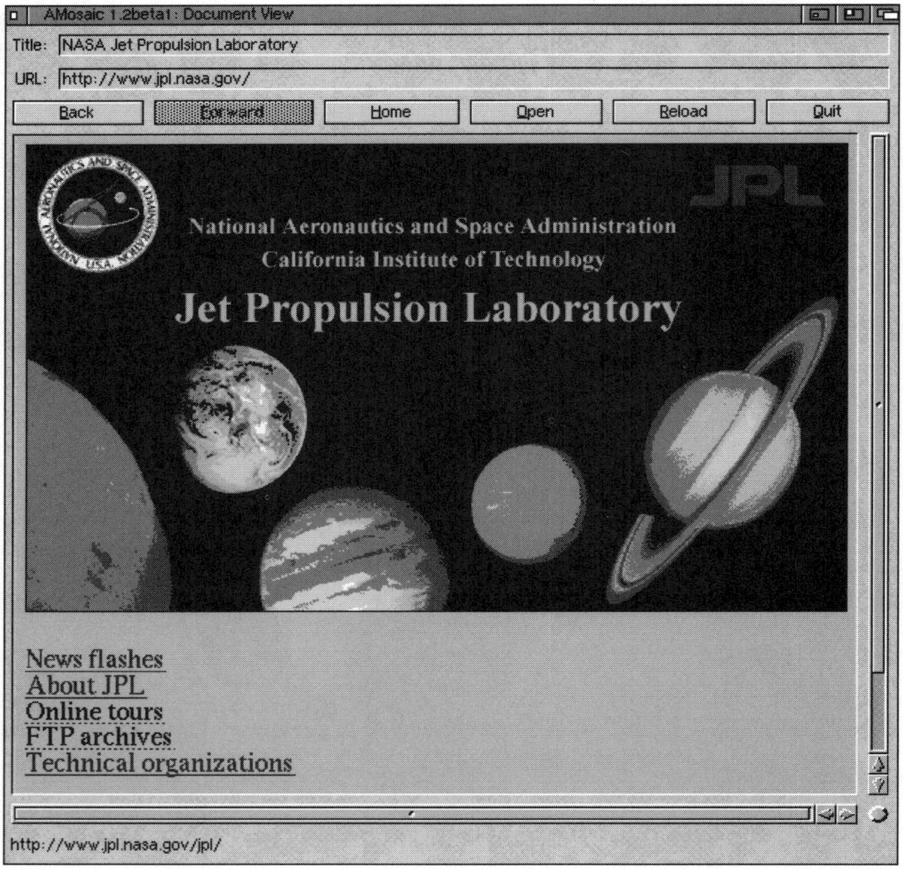

Figure 10.1 *NCSA Mosaic is available for most GUI computers, including the Amiga. This shot was taken with an Amiga 1200.*

If you go back through some of the early hobbyist computer magazines you'll find that a lot of journalists were getting very hot under the collar about something called Hypertext, as long ago as the early 1980s. Hypertext was going to revolutionize the way that computer users were presented with information – because a single document could provide links to other documents and services. If this chapter were a Hypertext document you would be able to click on 'Doom', either to pick up a brief description of what Doom is, or to go on to shoot up aliens (or whatever they are) with a shotgun. If it were a good implementation of the Hypertext concept, you'd be able to leave Doom running in a window and go on to knock up a few sales figures in Visicalc, or spread abuse on IRC, all at the same time. Your Hypertext browser would leave the links to the original document in place so you could pop back at a moment's notice without having to reload the images or the text.

The technology to make Hypertext hum along didn't really start to become available until the end of the 1980s, by which time Visicalc was just a fond memory. (Many of today's Internetters and personal computer users won't know what part Visicalc played in the history of personal computer-ing.) But Hypertext has found its place as a navigation and search tool for the Internet, and the World Wide Web is flavour of the month, mainly because it uses a decidedly handsome piece of client software to let users wander around the Internet.

W3 – the World Wide Web (WWW)

Development on what was to become the WWW was started in 1980 by a guy called Tim Berners-Lee working at the CERN complex. His Hypertext system was designed in isolation from other budding Hypertext software, but became the focus of a system designed to ship information around between particle physics scientists. Early client software for WWW was character based but the National Center for Supercomputing Applications (NCSA) stepped in and designed GUI based WWW browser clients for Mac, Windows and X-Windows. These browser clients are probably one of the main reasons that WWW is so popular. Today it's reported that there's a new WWW server appearing on the 'Net every day.

WWW uses the Hypertext metaphor to present information. You access it through a GUI client like NCSA's Mosaic, or Cello, or you can get at it via telnet and one of the character based clients such as Lynx. The character based clients aren't of much interest to the current generation of Amiga, Mac or Windows users, because WWW provides a rich feed of graphics and sounds in addition to text based information. You click on an icon and a picture (eventually) appears, or a sound erupts. The graphics and sound handling is provided by the graphics and sound handling programs you have on your computer; the WWW client serves only to hook information into your machine's software support routines and

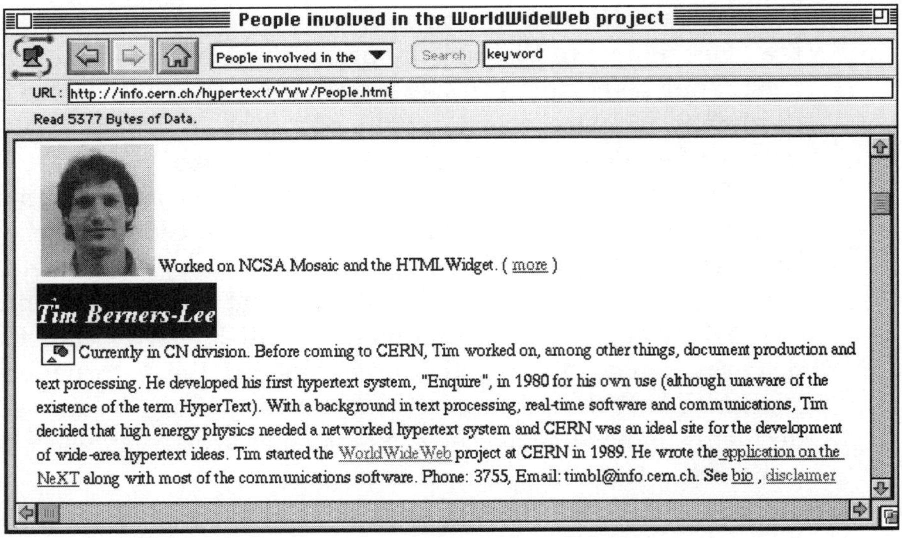

Figure 10.2 *Tim Berners-Lee, father of the World Wide Web. You get his biography, including photo, from the Web itself.*

display hardware. If you use telnet to get to WWW pages you won't be able to get the graphics files, which is yet another major reason to go for a full Internet connection, especially if you think that you'll ever want to get sound and vision from the 'Net.

NCSA Mosaic

Mosaic is currently one of the most widely used WWW browsers, probably because it's free, and probably because it works. You use Mosaic to navigate around Internet resources by point-and-clicking on links or pointers to other services. These have HTTP addresses (Hypertext Transport Protocol) which are resolved by the TCP/IP connection to take you straight to the site containing the relevant data. This method of navigation supersedes all other methods of rummaging around the Internet – it provides a seamless way of getting from server to server, and country to country, without the technology of navigation or the complexities of UNIX getting in the way. You'll see the HTTP addresses appear in the status bar of Mosaic, if you have this option turned on.

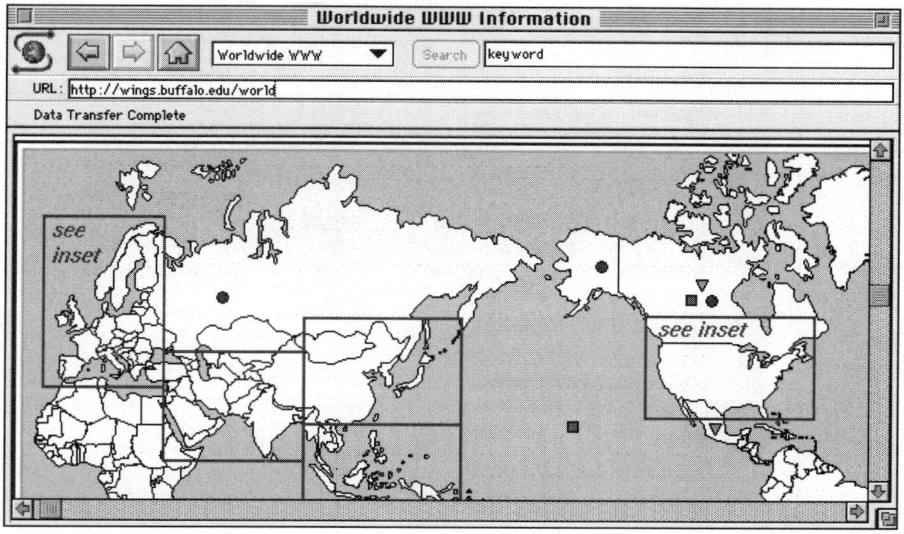

Figure 10.3 *A lesson on the death of the UNIX command line interface. Clicking on a region brings up a list of countries as fast as your modem can shift the data.*

Mosaic lets you select a 'home page' to which you'll always be taken when you start the software up, although you can change this to any other page you wish. (The home page is a bit like the default Gopher server you are taken to when you start up a Gopher client.) You start to navigate by clicking on text links, which appear in blue, or underlined, or both. Once you've been to that link, the text for the link turns red and may be cached in your computer's memory to speed up access if you return. You can click on picture icons to see graphics files displayed on screen – like a colour magazine page. Pages already received are cached into memory or to disk, which means that Mosaic can run adequately over a fast modem link. ('Fast' in this case means a modem to V32 bis standards.) You can also grab pages and save them to disk, either as text files or as Mosaic native files. The latest versions of Mosaic are commonly available on the 'Net, especially from the NCSA server at ***ftp.ncsa.uiuc.edu***.

As we've seen with Gopher and Veronica, and with WAIS, your ability to navigate around the Internet is limited by the capability of the client programs or server based utilities that you use to find data. Just as Gopher supersedes Archie, so WWW supersedes

Figure 10.4 *The NCSA home page. It tells you where to get the latest browser software for your computer. Mosaic's built-in FTP client lets you download them off the page.*

Gopher and Veronica because it will hook seamlessly into Gopher or WAIS servers if the link appears to take you there. You don't have to know about the technicalities of the Internet to make use of it, which is why WWW is so important to non-technical users. It's the first real tool (or maybe the second after the GUI Gopher clients) for traipsing around the Internet which doesn't demand a grounding in UNIX before it can be used.

The best way to find out about the World Wide Web is to jump straight onto it. You'll need a WWW browser such as Mosaic (for Mac, Windows, Amiga) or Cello (Windows). You then log in to your Internet provider as usual and fire up the browser. Mosaic needs no pre-configuration. You'll be able to navigate around the menus with ease. If you are running a slow modem then look for a menu option to 'Display URLs' (uniform resource locators). Deselect this before you start and the graphic images will not be sent to you unless you click on the icons.

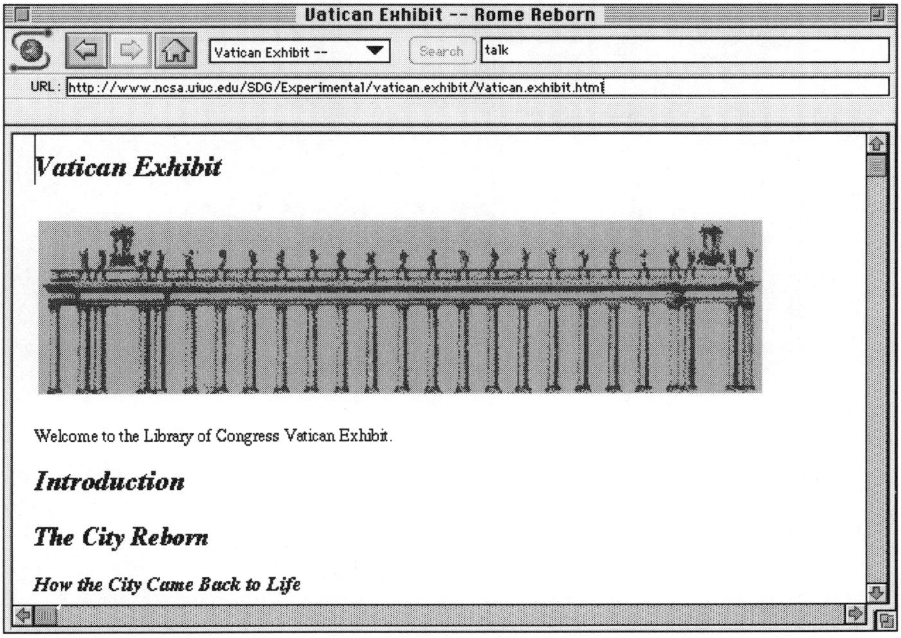

Figure 10.5 *Is the Pope an Internet provider? The Vatican Library on the World Wide Web.*

Service providers and HTML

HTML is the Hypertext markup language used to construct pages for the World Wide Web. It's simple to master, and full details can be found on the Web itself. There are a number of utilities which let users construct pages in Microsoft Word, and other word processors. HTML is proving to be a great way of providing information, via the Web. New servers pop up every day, and many Internet providers will rent out space on their Web servers to almost anyone. This means that the Web has suddenly become the *de facto* standard for electronic mass picture and text publishing, and there are many interesting publications available as a result.

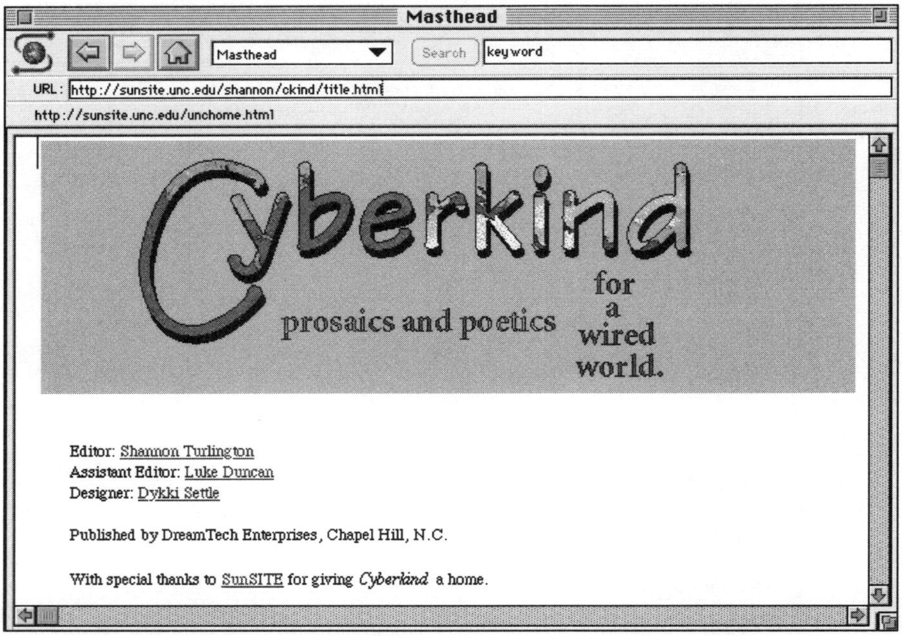

Figure 10.6 *Add 'cyber' as a prefix to anything and you're assured of instant nerdiness. Even poetry is a target.*

Again, the sheer variety of information on the Web defeats the ability of this book to display even a small proportion of it and you're therefore recommended to download a Web client from ***ftp.ncsa.uiuc.edu*** and fire it up. You'll be delighted with what you see – especially if you have a Mac, Windows or Amiga computer.

Figure 10.7 is from the WWW startup pages and will be out of date by the time we go to publication simply because the WWW is reputed to be expanding at the rate of 350 000 per cent per annum. But the file shows a little of what's available, to whet your appetite. With the real thing accessed via Mosaic or Cello you can click on any of the bulleted items and be taken to another document, which in turn will provide links to other servers and files. If you want a file to be sent to you then WWW will FTP it to you automatically; if you hook into a WAIS server then WWW will provide you with a transparent interface to the WAIS server via telnet. And you can get to all the Gopher services through WWW.

WWW is currently recognized as the 'killer application' that Internet providers have been waiting for. Access to the Web is being

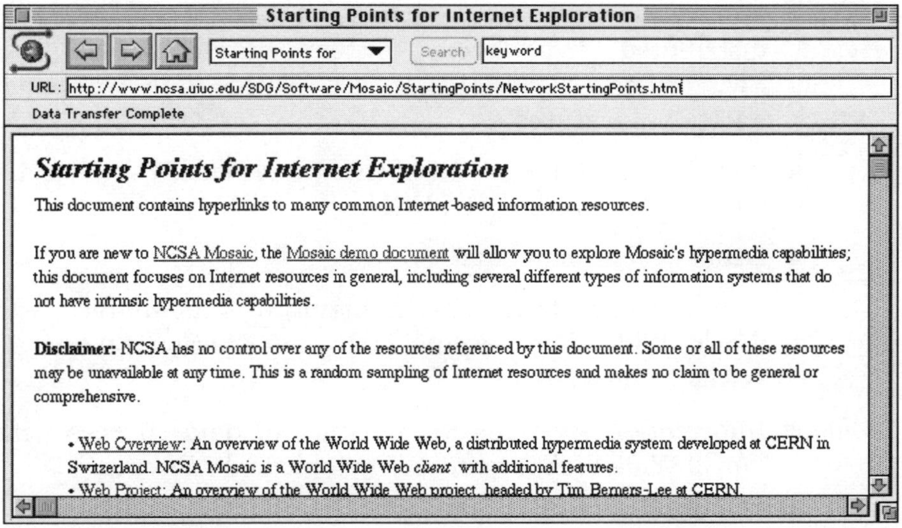

Figure 10.7 *The 'Starting Points' document. Clicking on a site takes you directly there. The document is updated frequently.*

touted as the easiest way to get to most of the Internet services, and providers are distributing Mosaic client software on the basis that it's all you need to start working with the 'Net. In many cases they may be right, although not all Internet services are currently available via WWW. But it may well be the case that WWW provides all the information you need, in one simple-to-use package.

Happy hunting!

Favourite places

The 'Starting Points for WWW Exploration' document contains hyperlinks to many common Internet based information resources.

If you are new to NCSA Mosaic, the original Mosaic demo document will allow you to explore Mosaic's hypermedia capabilities, whilst the 'Starting Points for WWW Exploration' document focuses on Internet resources in general, including several different types of information systems that do not have intrinsic hypermedia capabilities. What follows is a text version of the 'Starting Points' document, which is regularly updated.

- Web Overview: An overview of the World Wide Web, a distributed hypermedia system developed at CERN in Switzerland. NCSA Mosaic is a World Wide Web client with additional features.
- Web Project: An overview of the World Wide Web project, headed by Tim Berners-Lee at CERN.
- Other Web Documents
- Data Sources By Service: A listing of data sources within the World Wide Web, organized by information service (Gopher, WAIS, and so on).
- Information By Subject: A listing of data sources within the World Wide Web, organized by topic and subtopic.
- Web News: The latest World Wide Web news bulletin.
- Web Servers Directory: The central listing of known World Wide Web servers. Servers not yet registered with this list may be noted in the Mosaic 'What's New' list.
- InterNIC InfoGuide : A Web server run by the InterNIC; this is a good place to find general Internet-related information.
- NCSA Mosaic Home Page: The document NCSA Mosaic accesses upon start-up by default; this document tells you what the latest released version of NCSA Mosaic is at any given time.
- NCSA Mosaic Demo Page: A self-guided tour of the hypermedia capabilities of NCSA Mosaic.
- NCSA Mosaic 'What's New' Page: A day-by-day listing of new information resources on the Internet available through NCSA Mosaic.
- NCSA Doc Finder: Quick search-and-jump to any HTML documents on NCSA's web server.
- NCSA Home Page: The home page for the National Center for Supercomputing Applications at the University of Illinois at Urbana-Champaign.
- Other Home Pages: These are some interesting home pages located all around the world. For the complete listing of home pages, see the Web Servers Directory; for new home pages, see the Mosaic 'What's New' page.

- ANU Bioinformatics
- British Columbia
- BSDI Home Page
- Carnegie Mellon
- CERN Home Page
- Cornell Law School
- Cornell Theory Center
- DESY Home Page
- Honolulu Home Page
- Indiana Computer Science Home Page
- National Center for Atmospheric Research
- Northwestern Home Page
- Ohio State Home Page
- Pittsburgh Supercomputing Center Home Page
- SSC Home Page
- WAIS Starting Point: WAIS (Wide Area Information System) is a powerful searching engine in use over the Internet. This document tells you how to access WAIS servers through NCSA Mosaic.
- Gopher: Gopher is a popular menu-based information system in use on the Internet.
- GopherSpace Overview: A comprehensive listing of all the known Gopher servers in the world, organized by continent.
- Veronica: Veronica is a way to search 'Gopherspace' for specific pieces of information.
- NCSA Gopher: The Gopher server for the National Center for Supercomputing Applications.
- CTC Gopher: The Gopher server for the Cornell Theory Center.
- PSC Gopher: The Gopher server for the Pittsburgh Supercomputer Center.
- SDSC Gopher: The Gopher server for the San Diego Supercomputer Center.

- Original (UMN) Gopher: The Gopher server at the University of Minnesota, home of Gopher.
- UIUC Gopher: The central Gopher server at the University of Illinois at Urbana-Champaign.
- UIUC Weather Machine: The Weather Machine contains up-to-the-minute forecasts and weather satellite images.
- USC Math Gopher: The Gopher server for the University of South Carolina Department of Mathematics.
- FTP Sites: This is a comprehensive listing of anonymous FTP sites. This listing is not being actively maintained; it is provided as a proof-of-concept. We encourage others to maintain such a listing and make it available to the network.
- Usenet Newsgroups: This is a comprehensive listing of Usenet newsgroups available at CERN, where the listing is housed. This listing is not entirely appropriate for sites other than CERN; it is referenced here to encourage individual sites to set up such listings themselves.
- Finger Gateway: This is a gateway to Finger, a common utility program used to obtain information about people on the Internet.
- HyTelnet Gateway: This is a gateway to HyTelnet, a comprehensive index of publicly-accessible electronic library catalogs.
- TeXinfo Gateway: This is a gateway to a large collection of TeXinfo documents at Ohio State University.

Other information resources

- Hyper-G Gateway: Hyper-G is another Internet-based hypermedia system; this gateway is located in Austria.
- TechInfo Gateway: Techinfo is another Internet-based information system (somewhat like Gopher).
- X.500 Gateway: X.500 is an Internet-based phone book service.
- Whois Gateway: Whois is another Internet-based phone book service.

Other documents

Here are some additional interesting information resources not listed above that may interest people exploring the Internet.

- ANU Art History Exhibit: An exhibit of art history materials collected and put online by Michael Greenhalgh at Australian National University.
- Bryn Mawr Classical Review: BMCR is a review of classical literature distributed over the Internet.
- CyberNet: the central online 'jumping off' point for alternative information seekers. Their library of topics range from the bizarre, to the downright scary. If you're after information about anarchy, Nirvana, or goofy art, come on over.
- Electronic Visualization Lab: An exhibit of work done at the Electronic Visualization Lab at the University of Illinois at Chicago.
- Internet Services List: A standard list of Internet services collected by Scott Yanoff. (NB – doesn't cost $500 (Author))
- Internet Talk Radio: A collection of radio programs from Internet Talk Radio – because asynchronous times demand asynchronous radio.
- Library of Congress Vatican Exhibit: An exhibit of materials from the Vatican Library.
- Los Alamos Physics Papers (Gopher): The Gopher based interface to a central repository of physics papers at Los Alamos.
- Los Alamos Physics Papers (Web): The Web based interface to a central repository of physics papers at Los Alamos.
- NCSA Access Magazine: A hypermedia version of NCSA Access, a general-interest magazine published by the National Center for Supercomputing Applications.
- Postmodern Culture: Postmodern Culture is an edited journal distributed over the Internet.
- Unified CS Tech Reports: A central index of computer science technical reports from all around the world.

- White House Papers: A WAIS server containing all of the papers from the Clinton Administration from Day 1 to about two days ago.
- Internet RFCs: An archive of Internet Request for Comments documents, the technical documentation of the Internet.
- Zippy The Pinhead: Asynchronous irreverence.

UK information servers by name

Anglia Polytechnic University: ULTRALAB an experimental server of ULTRALAB software and information; general interest stuff; experimental areas. ULTRALAB is a learning technology research centre, so the server will be of particular interest to everyone in the learning/teacher training/educational software fields.

Apollo Advertising: A commercial server holding advertisers' WWW documents.

University of Bath: General information about the University of Bath. (Still under development.)

BBC : This is the BBC Networking Club WWW server.

Bulletin Board for Libraries (BUBL) Information Service: Including BUBL's Academic Information Service, Library and Information Science on BUBL and the GALLERY – a long (unsorted) list of interesting Web links.

The University of Birmingham: The School of Computer Science, degree and course programmes, current research details and information about the School of Computer Science. Also a Birmingham visitors' guide and other local information.

Brunel University: The Computer Centre/Brunel Library and Information Service (BLIS), information about the staff, faculties and library, including local area maps. There is also the Student Server.

University of Cambridge (UoC): University of Cambridge Computer Laboratory maintains links to all known Cambridge information servers:

UoC Institute of Astronomy, Royal Greenwich Observatory and Mullard Radio Astronomy Observatory.

UoC School of Biological Science. This server provides a wide variety of links to useful information resources for biologists. In addition, it supports a BLAST gateway for sequence database similarity searching.

UoC Cambridge Crystallographic Data Centre. Provides information relating to the Cambridge Structural Database System, including documentation in HTML format. Also a slowly growing postcard collection.

UoC Centre for Atmospheric Science (Chemistry). Provides information relating to the Centre (general info, seminars, publications and so on), information on the UK Universities Global Atmospheric Modelling Programme (general, data, software) via links to the anon.ftp server at caesar.atm.ch.cam.ac.uk.

UoC Engineering Department. Contains links to many other information sources relevant to control around the world, including ftp servers and Web servers containing technical reports and papers. It also contains some recent papers and PhD theses by members of the control group here. We have the first coffee machine on the Web so you can see how full it is and hence whether it is worth visiting it.

City University: The City University, London. Contains links to other services and maps of the area and the campus. 'Computer Science' contains information about the department and the School of Informatics.

CityScape Internet Services Ltd: Guides to CityScape products, their headquarters and their newsletter. Also their pub guide for Cambridge.

Cranfield University: University Postgraduate prospectus, Research Directory, and local information on computing services.

Demon Internet Services: Provides information on services and products for sale.

Durham University: Department of Mathematical Sciences. Information and links of general interest to Mathematicians / Theoretical Physicists / Statisticians.

University of Exeter: The Department of Computer Science has research papers, postgraduate study details and personnel information.

University of East Anglia:

School of Mathematics. This contains information about both the school and Ocean Modelling. The server is officially mandated by the department.

School of Information Systems. This contains information about the school including its staff.

Edinburgh University (EU): The main Computing Services server provides a hypertext of helpful information for new users of the UNIX operating system.

EU Chemical Engineering Department. Information about the department, its teaching, research and people.

EU Tardis Public-Access Service. A free, networked public-access UNIX service hosted by the Department.

Frontline Distribution Ltd: Frontline are one of the UK's largest TRADE distributors of computer hardware, software and services to the UK's computer reseller community.

HEPDATA: The HEPDATA High-Energy Physics database of published numerical results organized by Mike Whalley.

Hillside Systems & Berkeley Software Design International (Europe): The server at Hillside has technical information and a European order form for the BSD/386 UNIX-like operating system for 386, 486 and Pentium PCs. BSD/386 hypertext manual pages and a current patch set for BSD/386 V1.1 are also available. You can use anonymous FTP to get the data too. You will find a full list of titles for Peter Collinson's SunExpert and EXE articles.

Institute of Chartered Accountants of England and Wales, Accounting Information Service: The 'Summa' Project. This is the site of a World Wide Web information server for Accounting Academics, students and professionals. The service is funded by a grant from the Research Committee of the ICAEW. It is at present sited at the University of Exeter, Devon, UK. The Director of the project is Mr Barry J. Spaul.

Imperial College, University of London:

Department of Computing. Has information about the department and the src.doc.ic.ac.uk archive services (includes Archie scanning), the current UK weather and links to all other departmental WWW and other IC information servers.

Centre For Computing Services. Offers information about IC, computing facilities, and other local information.

Department of Chemistry. For details of this department, its staff, facilities and courses. Includes WATOC World Association of Theoretical Organic Chemists.

Theoretical Physics Group. The server contains information on the IC Theoretical Physics Group, as well as links to an FTP server containing recent preprints from members of the group. There are also a number of links to sites of interest to Theoretical Physicists, including all the known UK Theoretical Physics Groups. We also include all the known servers at Imperial College.

Solid State Theory Group.

Space and Atmospheric Physics Group.

Kingston University: This is a new, experimental, service.

Leeds University:

Computer-based learning unit

School of Chemistry

University Computing Service

Central Administration. This is the front page for the Administration web server, and leads to corporate, research and teaching information; this area is growing rapidly.

Loughborough University: High Performance Networks and Distributed Systems archive.

Mac-Supporters: Frequently asked questions (FAQs) and other assorted material related to supporting Apple Macintoshes.

Mailbase: Mailbase is the national electronic mailing list service for the UK academic and research community. It runs over 500 lists on a wide range of subjects with over 40,000 subscribers. The Mailbase WWW allows access to the archives and memberships of the public lists on the system.

University of Manchester: Manchester Computing Centre will shortly be used for the Central NRS (Name Registration Scheme) database.

Computer Graphics Unit. Computer Graphics services, software, research, images, computer graphics and scientific visualization information. Officially mandated and representative of the CGU.

Computer Science Department Feb 94. Small setup but growing.

University of Newcastle:

Theory of Condensed Matter Group, Dept. of Physics.

Arjuna Project Information. This server provides information about Arjuna, an object-oriented programming system that provides a set of tools for the construction of fault-tolerant distributed applications.

NEXUS: A server for NEXUS, the UK network of student physics societies.

Nexor: Includes full hypertext Archie gateways.

University of Nottingham:

Communications Research Group : Information on the Department of Computer Science and the Communications Research Group. Also includes an Archie gateway, and UK independent music scene information base.

University of Oxford:

Department of Earth Sciences. Access to departmental information plus links to other Oxford University information services.

PIPEX Ltd: The Public IP Exchange.

Rutherford Lab: The Rutherford Appleton Lab, UK. Admin: www-master@letterbox.rl.ac.uk.

SuperJANET: An information source of the UK SuperJANET project.

The University of Sheffield:

..is pleased to announce a WWW server based at its Academic Computing Services. Currently there is information from:

Department of Automatic Control & Systems Engineering.

Department of Chemistry. Features include WebElements: a periodic table of the elements database (this is the new permanent home for WebElements), an isotope pattern calculator (an interactive isotope patterns calculator – you supply the chemical formula), and an element percentage calculator (an interactive element percentage calculator – you supply the chemical formula).

The Hartlib Papers Project. News on the publication of the complete text and facsimiles of the Hartlib Papers.

Sheffield Collegiate Cricket Club. Information from Yorkshire's premier amateur cricket club.

University of Southampton:

Southampton High Energy Physics (SHEP). We have some local information and links to other High Energy Physics material.

Astronomy Group.

High Performance Computing Centre. The HPC Centre supports High Performance Computing within the South and South West of England. The Centre runs courses and workshops as well as supporting a number of HPC machines.

University of St Andrews, Scotland: The FIDE Project is part of a multi-site ESPRIT-funded project on database programming languages. This site provides information about project members and access to a number of papers about persistence and the database programming languages PS-algol and Napier88.

University of Strathclyde: This is run by the Computer Centre. Lists courses offered by the Centre, centrally managed clusters and contains links to other WWW servers on campus.

University of Surrey:

The Department of Electronic and Electrical Engineering. Contains information about the department and its reseach. Also EDUPAGE and Science Fiction TV series Guides .

University of Sussex:

School of Cognitive and Computing Sciences. This is a general information server about COGS. There is access to the anonymous FTP site giving access to COGS research papers. Also an index of the School's research papers, a calendar of Seminars and other events at the School. A gallery depicting members of the School.

University of Wales, College of Cardiff:

Department of Computing Mathematics (COMMA)

University of Ulster:

Faculty of Informatics. This server provides information on the staff and research interests of the Informatics Staff of the Faculty of Informatics at Coleraine. This information is officially mandated and is representative of our organization.

Warwick University:

WINFO WWW. Warwick Information WWW Service with lots of info about the University and things relating to it.

NURSE WWW. WWW Service for Nurses.

Law Technology WWW. Experimental service linking to other WWW/Gopher sites

UKOLN – The Office for Library and Information Networking: Links to various library related services.

University College, London:

Department of Computer Science including info on MICE (Multimedia Integrated Conferencing for European Researchers) and the MBONE (Multicast backBONE).

Part 3

Finale

11 A brief history of crime

'Anti-virus software
is a must for Internet
users...'

You may have gathered from the ten preceding chapters that there is a subculture of sorts permeating the Internet. It's this subculture which adopts self-styled titles like Cyberpunk, uses aliases instead of real names, and attempts to perpetuate the myth that, because the 'Net isn't controlled by a single authority, it therefore represents and provides anarchic freedom.

In fact the 'Net provides less freedom than the average democracy, as the contributors and users of the Internet impose their own conventions and restrictions on each other, much like the kids let loose in *Lord of the Flies*. A pecking order is established and those not deferring to it are penalized, just like in the real world. It's a bit like the joke which asks 'Which colour flag do anarchists use?' The answer is that anarchists have a black flag, but if they were really anarchists, they would all have different coloured flags.

The anarchist/hacker community represents only a small fraction of Internet users, but they shout with the loudest voice, presumably because they have the most to lose by the possibility of controls being placed on the Internet. The recent furore over the proposed Clipper encryption scheme, where US Government bodies proposed the adoption of a data encryption scheme to which they had a back-door key, is a case in point. It's the hackers and 'freedom fighters' on the 'Net who most dispute the point of having a Government sponsored encryption scheme. The average Joe in the street neither uses nor cares about encryption because he has nothing to hide – or more likely, he hasn't yet found the need to protect himself from the CIA or the National Security Agency.

But Joe's computers are under attack, or they soon will be. Hackers and virus writers currently cost US business hundreds of millions of dollars a year in downtime. Phone phreakers and call-whistlers consume a few more million dollars of revenue and keep the cost of calls to genuine users higher than they should be. Hacking, antisocial behaviour and using the Internet as a convenient route into and out of other people's computer systems is considered acceptable to many Internet users on the basis that if you're stupid enough to leave the doors open then you should expect people to walk in.

The reasons for hacking can be found in the various issues of 'Phrack', a hacker-based electronic newsletter scattered around the 'Net. You can get it by Gophering for it. Phrack is a contraction of phreaking and hacking, where phreaking is the gentle art of manipulating telecomms systems. Issues are studded with phrases such as 'vengeance', 'revenge', and 'corporate stupidity', and with opprobrium for those who try to control those involved. Judging from the pages of 'Phrack', the hacker mentality seems based on the male desire for control and power – and the Internet, with its wide-open availability of systems connected to it, provides rich pickings for data-rape.

Of late, hackers have tried to claim some small immunity from being lumped in with the rest of the break and enter community, and now claim that hacking is a legitimate exercise in self-progression and the gaining of technical knowledge. Hackers claim that it's 'cracking' that consists of breaking into computer or other systems with malicious intent, whereas 'hacking' is a mere intellectual pastime. In fact both hacking and cracking are now illegal in the UK courtesy of Emma Nicholson's Computer Misuse Act, a fine example of knee-jerk legislation which mainly serves to keep policemen out of other people's computer systems.

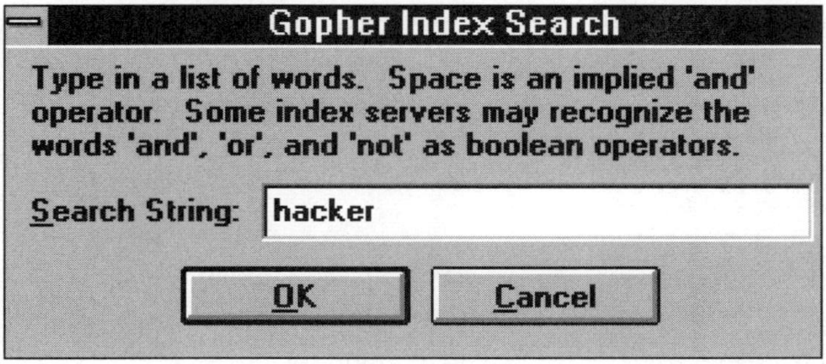

Figure 11.1 *Think hacking is a minority sport? A Gopher search for 'hacker' reveals much...*

How they do it

The transport tools of computer hackers are often the open systems run by educational sites and government computers. The chief means of entry is telnet, which, if you can find a port that takes you out of the public areas into private sections, will then let you telnet from that computer into others scattered all over the world. The most notorious hacks, including those documented in Clifford Stoll's *Cuckoo's Egg*, were carried out by logging into a relatively local site via a modem and humble terminal emulation package, and then using the telnet or 'rlogin' client on the host machine to loop around the Internet sites. The technique is simple – you don't even need TCP/IP software to achieve it, and many of the most infamous UK hacks have been carried out using nothing more exotic than a BBC computer and a 300 baud modem. One favourite tool of the early hackers was the Tandy 100 laptop, which included a built-in terminal emulator and modem and can be seen in pictures from many of the early UK telecomms magazines. In recent years the GNS packet switch network has provided a fine transport mechanism for hackers. Packet switch networks make it possible to dial a local number in most major towns to connect to systems anywhere in the world. And if the hacker gains access to a 'reverse-billing site' his unknowing host will be billed for the privilege. This small irony is not lost on many hackers. Packet switch networks also make it exceedingly difficult for phone numbers to be traced,

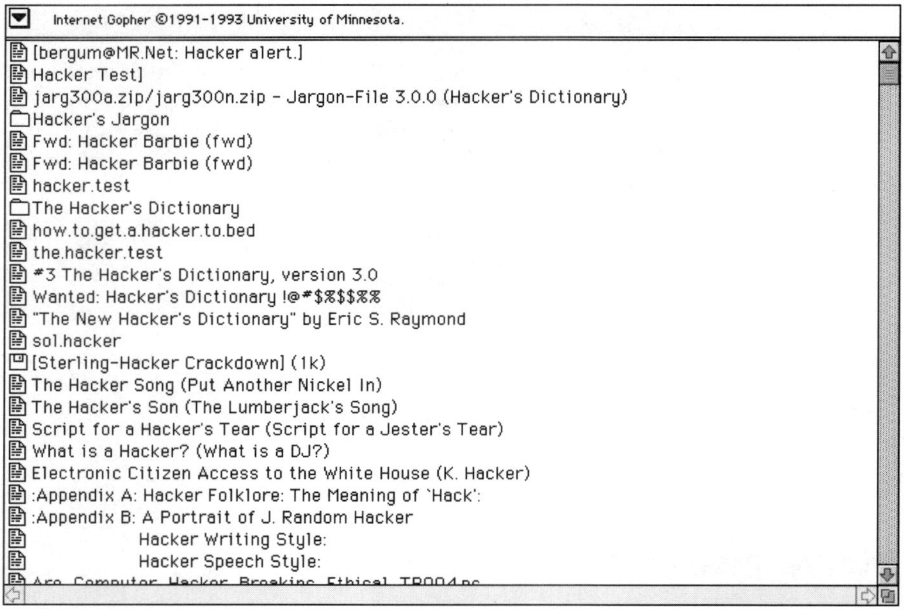

Figure 11.2 *This search revealed over a thousand hacker-related topics.*

as special technical knowledge and equipment is needed to trace packets back to the originating public dial-up node. Consequently many hackers now make exclusive use of the world's packet networks to avoid detection.

There may also be an element of phreaking involved in many hacks – especially in the USA where phone phreaking was a national hobby amongst students during the early to mid 1980s. Steve Jobs and Steve Wozniak founded what was to become Apple Computer on the strength of their expertise in making Blue Boxes – small boxes of electronics which could whistle their way across the world's telephone networks for free. Phreaking is still common in countries like Holland and the USA and to a lesser extent in Germany, but many hackers find it easier to steal credit card numbers and use them either to pay account bills, or to open accounts on commercial dial-up systems. Many systems allow new users to sign up with a credit card whereupon they are given full access, and virtually all of the UK's main systems providers have been caught out by bogus IDs backed up by stolen credit card numbers. Prime times for the activity are weekends and Bank

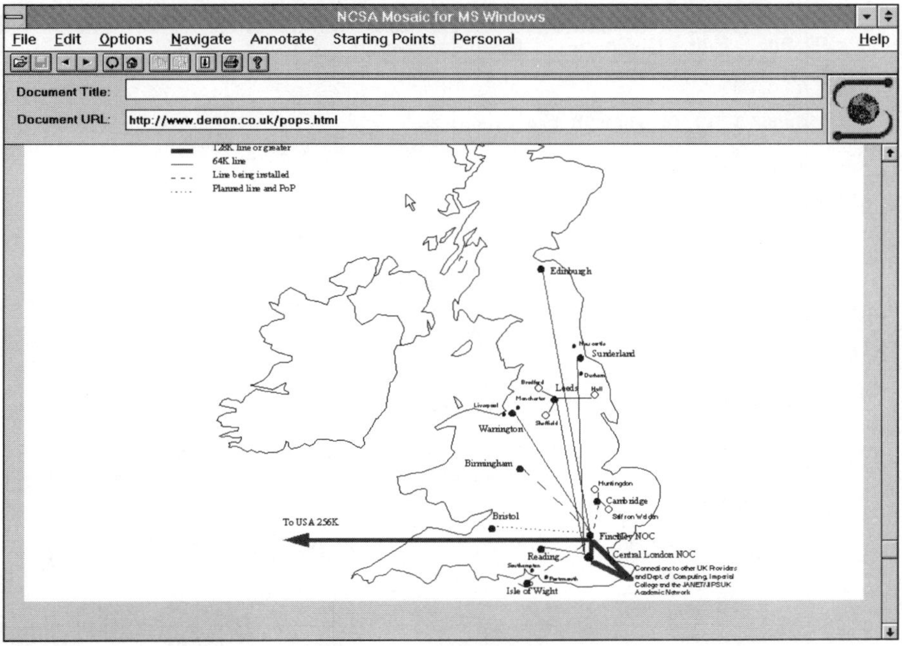

Figure 11.3 *Demon under attack? Telnet and remote login let hackers roam freely around the Internet.*

Holidays, when staff who would normally check card details are absent.

Many telnet sites have now tightened up security, but as soon as one door shuts, several more seem to open. Despite the publicity surrounding the Great Prestel Hack of 1984 in which hackers raided Prince Philip's Prestel Mailbox amongst other sites (two were prosecuted but acquitted – a third is alleged to have gone to ground), Nick Whiteley, a 19-year-old computer operator, managed to hack around many of Britain's top ICL sites, using an alias of 'The Mad Hacker' and a Commodore Amiga computer. Whiteley was able to get into systems and capture System Manager status, which then allowed him almost unlimited control of the computers. The question, of course, is why a 19-year-old, armed only with a decent brain and what's considered to be a toy computer by many contemporary computer writers, was able to cause so much disruption. The answer lies in the hopelessly inadequate precautions taken by software providers and designers to keep computer data from prying eyes.

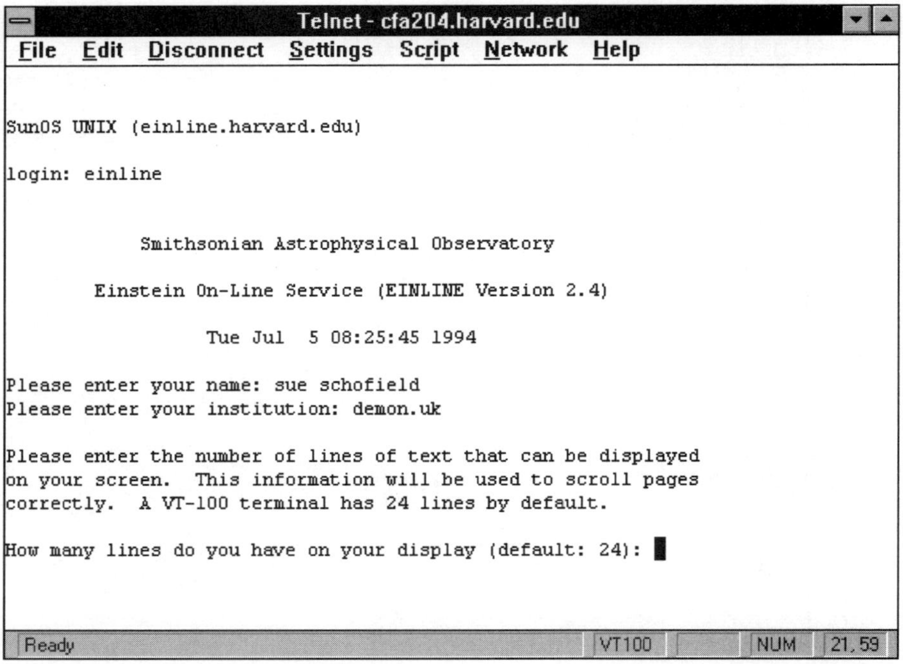

Figure 11.4 *Does telnet let almost anyone in? It can do, if the correct security precautions aren't in place.*

The corporate PC

Take a look at the Windows PC on your desk, for instance. You've read all the magazine articles and installed an anti-virus package, you've enabled the BIOS password protection, and you have password-protected your Word Perfect files and your spreadsheet data. That's about as far as the average corporate user goes. But there's a back door built into the BIOS of your PC which you don't know about. Anyone can get around the BIOS password feature supplied on millions of low price PCs, by holding down the INS key during a cold start.

And those password-protected word processor files? The last time you worked on those files, copies of them or the password used to encrypt them were probably stored in the hidden Windows swapfile on your disk. They are still stored there now as easily readable text unless you've been doing enough work on your PC to overwrite them. And if you've overwritten them, you may have left the imprint of something else – the password you used to access your company file server, or the letter you sent to the boss (or your lover?). It matters not if your data is stored on a distant file server, your local hard disk will carry the imprint of data which has been used in your Windows session. Even if you've taken the data files off your PC, that single large swapfile can contain passwords for your spreadsheets, your word processing files and the dial-up services you use. I found passwords to three dial-up systems, plus the registration passwords for an expensive Windows application, in the swapfile on the PC used for the screen shots, for instance.

Much the same sort of thing applies to the big corporate computers, like the DECs and ICLs. There are back doors built into these systems which even the suppliers themselves don't know about, and it's these areas which are the targets of hackers. Back doors to the VMS and ICL operating systems have been used in major hacks, and as recently as June 1994 Hewlett Packard were releasing software patches to prevent unauthorized access to their larger computers. Most of the Internet providers in the UK have already been hacked to some degree, although you'll find it hard to get acknowledgement of this fact from them. If these experts are open to invasion, what chance does the average corporate stand? The reality is that it is the hacker mentality of much of the Internet which keeps corporates from flocking to it.

So is a connection to the Internet really the best thing for UK business to contemplate? The answer must be that it will suit some, and not others. The UK computer press prints weekly success stories about companies using the Internet to gain on the competition – but rarely features stories about the many companies which have disconnected themselves because of security issues. Like all things, there's give and take, and in many cases an Internet connection can bring huge benefits. But it has to be designed and managed properly from the start.

Staving off the invaders

Keeping hackers and virus writers at bay is a full-time occupation. The prime transport mechanisms for hackers and virus distributors are telnet, FTP, mail and the password utilities of UNIX. Telnet lets unauthorized users gain entry to the port on the host system where throwing the contents of an electronic dictionary at the password prompt will often gain access. Or it's possible to get into many telnet ports with a default maintenance or system manager password. If that doesn't work then it's often possible to find a loophole in the directory structure of the host via FTP, and in some cases download the user log or system files which contain the password information. Going the other way it's possible to upload files to certain systems which give the hacker access to the system files or high-level user privileges, and if you have gaps like this in your system's security then it's only a matter of time before they are found out. Mail programs like 'sendmail' have been used to run commands on remote servers (in much the same way as you might run an Archie search via mail). The sendmail program has long since been updated – but there are some sites which haven't installed the update. And the UNIX password utilities have been hacked in many cases, to present the user with a utility which not only logs them in to the server, but captures the username and password to a file for later collection.

A less technical but more effective technique is simply to steal passwords and IDs from existing users by rummaging through Windows swapfiles as described earlier. It's relatively easy to hook up covert modems or displays to the serial lines used to connect VAX and other terminals to terminal servers, a technique known as sniffing. Sniffing of one sort or another is employed by many IT managers to monitor cabling and other serial line errors. High-level passwords can often be picked up from directors' secretaries who tend to leave them on Post-It notes, or in desktop diaries. But it's reckoned by some that 85 per cent of all computer crime is carried out from within the organization, where passwords can be easily noted, and where tape operators and support personnel often have full supervisor access to networks, including the payroll servers.

Electronic mail is probably the best carrier of passwords and, as mentioned, it's relatively easy to set up a system to monitor TCP/IP packets and decode textual information from them. Before the revolution in GUI based mail clients it was common for the UNIX 'sendmail' utility to be used for mail (it still is in many academic and UNIX sites) and sendmail can be and has been hacked on many occasions. Morris used it to trigger the Internet Worm, which brought most of the Internet to a standstill in November, 1988. The Worm sought out the email address books of the recipient. It used these to mail more copies of itself around the

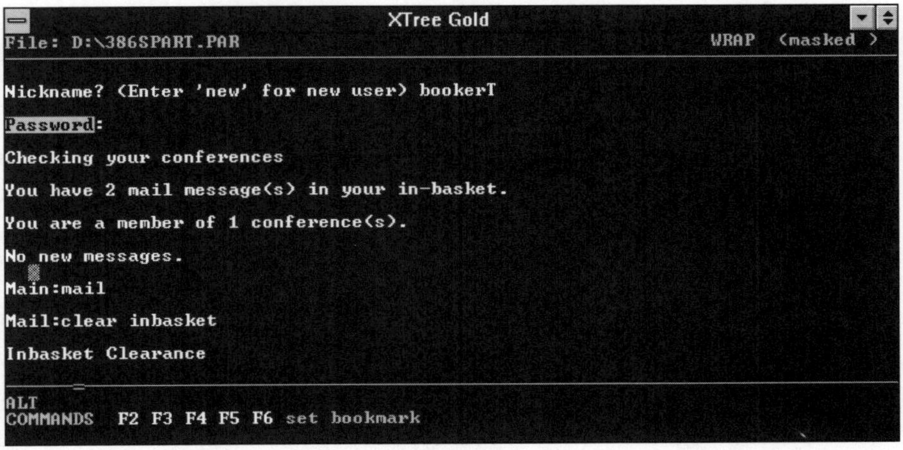

Figure 11.5 *Windows PCs are completely open to hackers. This particular log of a terminal session doesn't show the password, but if you can see it on the screen it will be saved in the Windows swapfile.*

Internet, growing larger (in the virtual sense) with each mail address it arrived at.

Future crime and the Internet

The level of hacker attacks is set to increase in the approach to the millennium, as more personal computers come into use, and the spread of personal internetworking continues. The techniques outlined in this chapter are public domain and common knowledge on the Internet – but not in many UK company environments where hacking is something we read about in the press but don't take much notice of. We even have the Computer Misuse Act which was intended to keep 'unauthorized' people out of computer systems. Alas, the Act is working too well: police are now effectively being kept out of private 'adult' dial-up systems by a simple login message which claims that they may not enter as they, the police, aren't 'authorized users'.

Viruses are a different matter. Anonymous FTP makes it easy

to inject viruses into a community of 20–30 million users, and I found two major virus releases during the time I researched this book. The first was a Trojan Horse loaded into a program which claimed to make CD-ROMs writable, the second was placed into copies of the well-known McAfee ***anti-virus*** software. I also used telnet to log into a system containing a virus library – where anyone may log in and grab viruses for either research or more nefarious use, and I was offered a CD-ROM containing the source code for many common viruses.

Uncorrupted anti-virus software is therefore a must for anyone thinking of downloading files from the Internet. As the Internet grows and develops it's going to become more difficult to protect against invasion of your personal and corporate systems. The World Wide Web, with its graphical pages, makes it exceptionally easy for viruses to be distributed, because in many cases your computer is downloading files without you realizing it. And both Archie and Gopher are capable of pointing you towards files which may be infected because they haven't been scanned by the system offering them for access.

Many notable computer evangelists are predicting the overrunning of the Internet by hackers and virus writers, but this may not happen. Governments are slowly transforming the Internet from an open academic institution into a privatized network, and funding for network provision is already being cut. It will take a few years, but the Internet is moving towards a controlled commercial base, where site security might just be taken as a serious topic. But there will always be people around who feel a need to take computer security of other people's systems as a personal challenge.

Moral? You must take precautions against invasion of your computer systems, regardless of size or cost, when you connect to the Internet.

12 Internet past, present and future

'In many cases the Internet is just a data dump...'

The Internet was created by the Pentagon's Advanced Research Projects Agency (ARPA) in the Kennedy era. The aim of ARPA was to bring together scientific minds to research and develop technology that would enable America to stay ahead in the Cold War. The guiding light in ARPA was Bob Taylor, a computer visionary who started trying to find better ways of working with computers while he was at NASA. Taylor eventually moved to the Defense Department and was one of the first founders of ARPA.

Taylor launched ARPA by setting up a number of research projects at American universities, and came up with the idea of ARPAnet, the very first transnational computer network. Its purpose was to link the scientists and researchers together. The technology used to transfer data between computers had been developed in the early sixties by Paul Baran, who was working on ways of preventing telephone systems from being destroyed by the electromagnetic pulse (EMP) effect during thermonuclear bomb blasts. Baran developed the first packet switching techniques, which were then incorporated into wide area network (WAN) technology. The firsts tests of NCP – Network Control Protocol – were carried out at Britain's National Physical Laboratory in 1968, and were successful enough to convince the Pentagon's Advanced Research Projects Agency to install the first nodes in 1969, creating ARPAnet. NCP was later superseded by TCP/IP.

ARPAnet operated using DEC PDP-10 computers and the message and data handling was carried out using separate minicomputers known as TIPs (terminal interface processors). The TIPs were linked to other TIPs over leased phone connections and the first nodes connected were the University of California at Los Angeles, Santa Barbara, the Stanford Research Institute, and the University of Utah.

By 1973 the ARPAnet had turned into a national network, but access to the system was limited to universities, research establishments, and defence contractors. The network operated with a great sense of wonder and there was no security anywhere on the system. Virtually any student (or friend of a student) who had access to a terminal connected to a TIP could log into any other computer, and spend hours or days cruising round its insides. Many of the academics who used the system found that electronic mail was much more interesting an application than mailing research papers around, and the beginnings of the social structure of the Internet emerged.

In 1975 the ARPAnet was turned over to the Defense Communications Agency, an organization dedicated mainly to overseeing military and government radio and data traffic. Security on the net was tightened somewhat, but to no great degree. The ARPAnet was at that time limited to 8-bit addressing techniques, which meant that no more than 256 sites could be connected directly at any one time. A new network addressing scheme was introduced in 1982, which meant that thousands of networks could be connected to each other, and the true Internet was born. ARPAnet split from the Internet in 1983 and became Milnet.

The growth of the Internet was rapid, and spread not only to research establishments, but to the corporate sector. In the early days the ARPAnet was used mainly for communications and data generated and sustained by research projects, but by the mid-1980s the Internet was becoming saturated with electronic mail from all corners of the world, including private individuals. This was anathema to those involved at the start, mainly because the costs of connecting to the Internet had dropped to the sort of levels where small corporations could afford connections. By the start of the 1990s it was estimated that the Internet carried over 2 million regular users, much to the chagrin of the universities and government departments who were directly funding the backbone of the service.

Birth of UNIX

In 1969 Ken Thompson, a worker at the Bell Laboratories Science Research Murray Hill labs, decided to invent UNIX. Thompson's idea was to write an operating system for his own use, one that would multitask, and eventually become virtually processor-independent. Thompson's project quickly caught the enthusiasm of co-workers and UNIX blossomed. Various universities also caught the bug, and many of the larger American faculties eventually developed their own implementations of Thompson's work.

UNIX was tailor-made for use on computer networks. Utilities such as ftp, Finger and sendmail became standards for accessing and using the computers connected to the Internet. The early UNIX implementations were often bug-ridden, because anyone and everyone had a hand in its development and there was no central coordination of development amongst the academics who used and 'improved' UNIX. In fact there were so many implementations of UNIX that it was possible to find different versions sitting on adjacent terminals in most of America's universities.

The combination of flaws in UNIX, the curious minds of students, an utter lack of security on the Internet, and the 'hacker mentality' led to huge problems for the Internet on many occasions. The arrival of cheap personal computers in 1982 started the explosion in Internet use. Almost any sort of computer can now be hooked up, as long as the TCP/IP software is available for it. TCP/IP is now truly multi-platform and it's often very difficult to tell just what type of computer is providing the service at the remote end of the link.

Present

The Internet has started to distend with new users in the mid-nineties. The huge sales of personal computers in the West is one reason, the availability of cheap telephone modems is another. It's estimated that there are 50 million personal computers in the USA, and about the same number in Western Europe, although less than a quarter of these are fitted with modems or network access of any kind. That gives a population of about 25 million modem users – about the same as some estimates for the number of Internet users in 1994 – although not all modem users have Internet access.

Hyperbole about the Internet is rife. It's dubbed the Information Superhighway, the InfoBahn, or the Digital Revolution, depending on the thickness of glossy paper your favourite computer magazine is printed on. Some of this might actually be true if you had an Ethernet connection to the Internet, but modems present the Digital Superhighway to the user as an information traffic jam, and few UK journalists seem to be plugged into the Internet over a network cable. Services like Internet Talk Radio demand transfers of files up to 30 megabytes in length, and are not realistically available to users of current modem technology, because of the download costs.

The Internet traffic snarl-up is unlikely to improve even with the arrival of V.34 modems, as there's always more data waiting to be downloaded than there is bandwidth available to get it. At the moment the theoretical bandwidth of modems over European networks is believed to be about 32 kilobits per second. This roughly equates to 2000 words of ASCII text per second, but it's likely that new transport techniques such as ATM will start to erode the supremacy of the analogue telephone modem.

It has to be said that access to the Internet over a phone line is cruddy. It's expensive because it takes a long time to squeeze large files down the limited bandwidth of modems, and it's frustrating because the same bandwidth limitations prevent you from doing something else on the same line while you're transferring data. Unfortunately, alternatives to dial-up access are expensive. A leased line with 64 Kbits per second, enough for a couple of heavyweight users, costs around £8000 per year to install and maintain, and the much-vaunted ISDN is still too expensive for the average punter to contemplate. But enter the Information Superhighway. The phrase itself comes from a visionary speech by Vice President of America Al Gore, and points towards a system of unlimited bandwidth connections direct to businesses and homes in the USA. It's envisaged that the network will be more or less complete in the first decade of the new millennium, bringing unlimited amounts of data and information to businesses, schools and homes. Things are not so clear in the UK and Europe. Over-regulation of telecomms providers is in place in the UK, which specifically forbids telcos (telecomms companies) from 'broadcasting'. This is to give the cable entertainment companies a head start, in return for the investment (and jobs) that the cable companies bring. While it's conceivable that cable will eventually carry Internet connections, the overall policy is short-sighted enough to ensure that Britain will lag behind the USA in information provision, unless policies are changed in the next year or so. Similar policies prevail in much of Europe, and despite Europe being the home of the much-vaunted ITU/U (ex CCITT), European telecomms are a mishmash of systems, technology and policy. The Information Superhighway will be a long time coming as a result.

Neither is the Internet the Information Repository. In many cases the Internet is a sort of data dump, where much useless trivia blocks access to the virtual shelves of pure knowledge. Consequently, you need to wade through an awful lot of garbage to get to real knowledge on the Internet. Alas, some pundits have even said that the Internet now contains all human knowledge, which is, of course, a sad joke.

As this chapter was being written British Telecom announced that it would be providing Internet access in the near future, which is welcome news for subscribers if not for Internet providers. Once the telcos – the telecomms providers – get involved it won't be long before the Internet is available at any phone line – as long as the bill continues to be paid.

The future

Anything written about the techno-future is doomed to be inaccurate. Two years ago I wrote that ISDN was the data transfer medium of the future, and two years later ISDN is still the consumer backwater it was then. High equipment prices and a lack of promotion by the telcos haven't helped, neither has the

Figure 12.1 *Even the BBC is tackling the Internet. It can't be that difficult after all.*

introduction of V.FAST and V.34 modems, which can run a megabyte a minute of text through ordinary phone lines. But there have been advances. Systems which offer video on demand have been demonstrated and there's currently a pan-European test to run ATM. ATM (asynchronous transfer mode) is a technology which allows virtually unlimited bandwidth to be made available over dial-up lines or Ethernet, and looks set to get here in about five years' time. The implications for Internet users are enormous and the promise of unlimited transmission bandwidth means that the only limitation to data transfer will be the speed at which your hard disk can write files. Data will consist of moving images, sound, and all of the stuff we now call multimedia, instead of the plain ASCII text which constitutes the vast majority of Internet traffic today.

The Internet is evolving to meet the future, or perhaps it's the other way around. Services like World Wide Web have become more sophisticated, and multimedia, Internet based voice-mail in real time, and elementary online video conferences are already here. The future, it would seem, holds unlimited promise for Internet users, and the writing is certainly on the wall for providers who continue to lope along with character based terminal interfaces. The days of typing arcane commands into a distant computer are now past, and many Internet providers are beginning to realize this. Some never will, and will slowly fade into the past, just like MS-DOS 2.1 did.

The future of the Internet is bright and multicoloured and doesn't demand that users scrabble with UNIX in order to be able to use it. At least that's how it looks from this end of a GUI.

Glossary

Distilled from RFC 1392, the *Internet Glossary*, and *The UK Internet Book*.

Acceptable Use Policy (AUP) Many transit networks have policies which restrict the use to which the network may be put. A well-known example is NSFNET's AUP which does not allow commercial use. Enforcement of AUPs varies with the network.

ACK See *acknowledgment.*

acknowledgment (ACK) A type of message sent to indicate that a block of data arrived at its destination without error. [Source: NNSC]

acoustic coupler Means of connecting external devices to a telephone handset avoiding direct electrical connection; most commonly used for low-speed data terminals.

AD See *administrative domain.*

address There are three types of addresses in common use within the Internet. They are email address; IP, internet or Internet address; and hardware or MAC address. See also: *email address, internet address, IP address.*

address mask A bit mask used to identify which bits in an IP address correspond to the network and subnet portions of the address. This mask is often referred to as the subnet mask because the network portion of the address can be determined by the encoding inherent in an IP address.

address resolution Conversion of an internet address into the corresponding physical address.

Address Resolution Protocol (ARP) Used to dynamically discover the low-level physical network hardware address that corresponds to the high-level IP address for a given host. ARP is limited to physical network systems that support broadcast packets that can be heard by all hosts on the network. It is defined in RFC 826.

administrative domain (AD) A collection of hosts and routers, and the interconnecting network(s), managed by a single administrative authority.

Advanced Research Projects Agency Network (ARPANET) A pioneering longhaul network funded by ARPA (now DARPA). It served as the basis for early networking research, as well as a central backbone during the development of the Internet. The ARPANET consisted of individual packet switching computers interconnected by leased lines. [Source: FYI4]

anonymous FTP Anonymous FTP allows a user to retrieve documents, files, programs, and other archived data from anywhere in the Internet without having to establish a user-id and password. By using the special user-id of 'anonymous' the network user will bypass local security checks and will have access to publicly accessible files on the remote system.

Archie A system to automatically gather, index and serve information on the Internet. The initial implementation of Archie provided an indexed directory of filenames from all anonymous FTP archives on the Internet. Later versions provide other collections of information.

archive site A machine that provides access to a collection of files across the Internet. An 'anonymous FTP archive site', for example, provides access to this material via the FTP protocol.

ARP See *Address Resolution Protocol*.

ARPANET See *Advanced Research Projects Agency Network*.

ASCII American Standard Code for Information Interchange. A standard character-to-number encoding widely used in the computer industry. ASCII is the standard used for sending non-binary messages over the Internet.

asynchronous Occurring without central control or in an unpredictable time interval between successive elements; the typical mode of telegraphy, minicomputers and personal computers; requires transmission of start and stop bits to provide decoding synchronization at the receiver.

Asynchronous Transfer Mode (ATM) A method for the dynamic allocation of bandwidth using a fixed-size packet (called a cell). ATM is also known as 'fast packet'.

ATM See *Asynchronous Transfer Mode*.

AUP See *Acceptable Use Policy*.

BABT British Approvals Board for Telecommunications. An independent body responsible for approval procedures for UK telecomms equipment. Only BABT-approved equipment may be connected to UK services, regardless of the supplier of these services.

backbone The top level in a hierarchical network. Stub and transit networks which connect to the same backbone are guaranteed to be interconnected.

baud A unit of signalling speed named after Baudot, who invented time division multiplexing in 1874. The speed in baud is the number of discrete conditions or signal elements per second. If each signal event represents only one bit condition, then baud is the same as bits per second. Baud does not otherwise equal bits per second. Baud rate is not applicable to contemporary modems equipped with data compression.

BBS See *bulletin board system*.

BinHex Program for the Macintosh computer which translates binary files into ASCII representations. Converted binary files can then be transferred as electronic mail. Used to get over the 7-bit limitations of the Internet.

bis 'Second Working' or 'Second Implementation' as used in CCITT recommendations.

Bitnet An academic computer network that provides interactive electronic mail and file transfer services, using a store-and-forward protocol, based on IBM Network Job Entry protocols. Bitnet-II encapsulates the Bitnet protocol within IP packets and depends on the Internet to route them.

bounce The return of a piece of mail because of an error in its delivery. [Source: ZEN]

bps 'bits per second' – describes the throughput of modems. Divide bits per second by ten to come up with an estimate of the number of characters per second (cps) transmitted.

bridge A device which forwards traffic between network segments based on datalink layer information. These segments would have a common network layer address.

bulletin board system (BBS) A computer, and associated software, which typically provides electronic messaging services, archives of files, and any other services or activities of interest to the bulletin board system's operator. Although BBSs have traditionally been the domain of hobbyists, an increasing number of BBSs are connected directly to the Internet, and many BBSs are currently operated by government, educational and research institutions.

Campus Wide Information System (CWIS) A CWIS makes information and services publicly available on campus via kiosks, and makes interactive computing available via kiosks, interactive computing systems and campus networks. Services routinely include directory information, calendars, bulletin boards, databases.

CCITT Comité Consultatif International des Téléphones et Télégraphes, a major constituent of the International Telecommunications Union (ITU) that sets standards for the operation of telecommunications services across international boundaries. Many CCITT recommendations are adopted for use domestically. Now renamed to 'ITU'.

CERT See *Computer Emergency Response Team.*

client A computer system or process that requests a service of another computer system or process. A workstation requesting the contents of a file from a file server is a client of the file server. [Source: NNSC]

client–server model A common way to describe the paradigm of many network protocols. Examples include the name-server/name-resolver relationship in DNS (domain name system) and the file-server/file-client relationship in NFS (network file system).

Computer Emergency Response Team (CERT) The CERT was formed by DARPA in November 1988 in response to the needs exhibited during the Internet worm incident. The CERT charter is to work with the Internet community to facilitate its response to computer security events involving Internet hosts, to take proactive steps to raise the community's awareness of computer security issues, and to conduct research targeted at improving the security of existing systems.

CR Carriage return. A control character causing the print or display position to move to the first position on the line, drawn from the typewriter and teleprinter function with similar action.

cracker (USA) A cracker is an individual who attempts to access computer systems without authorization. These individuals are often malicious, as opposed to 'hackers', and have many means at their disposal for breaking into a system.

CRC See *cyclic redundancy check.*

CWIS See *Campus Wide Information System.*

Cyberspace A term coined by William Gibson in his fantasy novel *Neuromancer* to describe the 'world' of computers, and the society that gathers around them. [Source: ZEN]

cyclic redundancy check (CRC) A number derived from a set of data that will be transmitted. By recalculating the CRC at the remote end and comparing it with the value originally transmitted, the receiving node can detect some types of transmission errors. [Source: MALAMUD]

DARPA See *Defense Advanced Research Projects Agency.*

data communications equipment (DCE) Standards-body term for devices that perform signal conversion at the extremities of a data circuit. A data set (modem) or a CSU are common examples of a DCE. Compare with *data terminal equipment.*

data encryption key (DEK) Used for the encryption of message text and for the computation of message integrity checks (signatures).

Data Encryption Standard (DES) A popular, standard encryption scheme.

data terminal equipment (DTE) The standards-body term for a computer, user terminal, workstation or personal computer used for data communications. Compare with *data communications equipment.*

DCE See *data communications equipment.*

DDN See *Defense Data Network.*

DDN NIC See *Defense Data Network, Network Information Center.*

Defense Advanced Research Projects Agency (DARPA) An agency of the US Department of Defense responsible for the development of new technology for use by the military. DARPA (formerly known as ARPA) was responsible for funding much of the development of the Internet we know today, including the Berkeley version of UNIX and TCP/IP. [Source: NNSC]

Defense Data Network (DDN) A global communications network serving the US Department of Defense composed of MILNET, other portions of the Internet, and classified networks which are not part of the Internet. The DDN is used to connect military installations and is managed by the Defense Information Systems Agency.

Defense Data Network Network Information Center (DDN NIC) Often called 'The NIC', the DDN NIC's primary responsibility is the assignment of Internet network addresses and AutonomousSystem numbers, the administration of the root domain, and providing information and support services to the DDN. It is also a primary repository for RFCs (requests for comments).

Defense Information Systems Agency (DISA) Formerly called the Defense Communications Agency (DCA), this is the government agency responsible for managing the DDN portion of the Internet, including the MILNET. Currently, DISA administers the DDN, and supports the user assistance services of the DDN NIC.

DEK See *data encryption key.*

DES See *Data Encryption Standard.*

dial-up A temporary, as opposed to dedicated, connection between machines established over a standard phone line.

digest Instead of getting email messages from your listserv subscription one at a time as they are posted, the digest format gives you a compilation of the day's (week's, month's) messages. Some folk prefer this format since it helps to manage a large influx of mail and helps hold discussion on a certain topic together. Others prefer the more immediate and spontaneous 'heat' of receiving messages as they are posted. Note: not all listservs offer this distribution option.

DISA See *Defense Information Systems Agency.*

DNS See *Domain Name System.*

domain 'Domain' is a heavily over-used term in the Internet. It can be used in the Administrative Domain context, or the Domain Name context.

Domain Name System (DNS) The DNS is a general-purpose distributed, replicated, data query service. The principal use is the lookup of host IP addresses based on host names. The style of host names now used in the Internet is called 'domain name', because they are the style of names used to look up anything in the DNS. Some important domains are: .COM (commercial), .EDU (educational), .NET (network operations), .GOV (US government), and .MIL (US military). Most countries also have a domain. For example, .US (United States), .UK (United Kingdom), .AU (Australia). It is defined in STD 13, RFCs 1034 and 1035.

DTE See *data terminal equipment.*

dweeb Slang (USA). Derogatory term for an unliked person, often young and unknowledgeable. Dweebs sometimes mature into *nerds*, and then into *geeks*.

EARN See *European Academic and Research Network*.

Ebone A pan-European backbone service.

EFF See *Electronic Frontier Foundation*.

e-journal Electronic journal. Newsletters, zines, periodicals, scholarly journals same as the hard copy, except available over the 'Net. You can access e-journals two ways: (1) a subscription will have the journal delivered to your email box, or (2) you can look up the journal at its host site (via WAIS or Gopher) and if you want a copy you can have it delivered via FTP.

Electronic Frontier Foundation (EFF) A foundation established to address social and legal issues arising from the impact on society of the increasingly pervasive use of computers as a means of communication and information distribution.

electronic mail (email) A system whereby a computer user can exchange messages with other computer users (or groups of users) via a communications network. Electronic mail is one of the most popular uses of the Internet. [Source: NNSC]

email address The domain-based or UUCP address that is used to send electronic mail to a specified destination.

emulate/emulation Imitating a system or device such that a connected device accepts the same information, executes the same computer programs and achieves the same results as if the emulator were one of its own kind. Most often, emulation is a downward step in the capability of the device being used, as when a personal computer is used to emulate a mechanical teleprinter or a 'dumb' terminal on a computer network. While some degree of upward emulation is possible, it is less prevalent in the broad view of computer communications.

encryption Encryption is the manipulation of a packet's data in order to prevent any but the intended recipient from reading that data. There are many types of data encryption, and they are the basis of network security.

error correction Used within modems (V42) to manage error-free comms.

Ethernet A 10 Mb/s standard for LANs (local area networks), initially developed by Xerox, and later refined by Digital, Intel and Xerox (DIX). All hosts are connected to a coaxial cable where they contend for network access using a Carrier Sense Multiple Access with Collision Detection (CSMA/CD) paradigm.

European Academic and Research Network (EARN) A network connecting European academic and research institutions with electronic mail and file transfer services using the Bitnet protocol.

FAQ Frequently Asked Question. Either a frequently asked question, or a list of frequently asked questions and their answers. Many Usenet news groups, and some non-Usenet mailing lists, maintain FAQ lists (FAQS) so that participants won't spend lots of time answering the same set of questions.

FARNET A non-profit corporation, established in 1987, whose mission is to advance the use of computer networks to improve research and education.

Federal Information Exchange (FIX) One of the connection points between the American governmental internets and the Internet.

file transfer The copying of a file from one computer to another over a computer network.

File Transfer Protocol (FTP) A protocol which allows a user on one host to access, and transfer files to and from, another host over a network. Also, FTP is usually the name of the program the user invokes to execute the protocol.

finger A program that displays information about a particular user, or all users, logged on the local system or on a remote system. It typically shows full name, last login time, idle time, terminal line, and terminal location (where applicable). It may also display plan and project files left by the user.

FIX See *Federal Information Exchange.*

flame A strong opinion and/or criticism of something, usually as a frank inflammatory statement, in an electronic mail message. It is common to precede a flame with an indication of pending fire (that is, FLAME ON!). Flame Wars occur when people start flaming other people for flaming when they shouldn't have.

flow control In data communications, the use of buffering and other mechanisms that operate to avoid data loss in case the receiver cannot keep up with the transmitter. The ASCII control characters X-ON and X-OFF are frequently used examples; they are returned in the reverse direction as an instruction for the sender to hold or restart held transmission.

For Your Information (FYI) A subseries of RFCs (requests for comments) that are not technical standards or descriptions of protocols. FYIs convey general information about topics related to TCP/IP or the Internet.

freenet Community-based bulletin board system with email, information services, interactive communications, and conferencing. Freenets are funded and operated by individuals and volunteers – in one sense, like public television. They are part of the National Public Telecomputing Network (NPTN), an organization based in Cleveland, Ohio, devoted to making computer telecommunication and networking services as freely available as public libraries. [Source: LAQUEY]

FTP See *File Transfer Protocol.*

FYI See *For Your Information.*

gateway The term 'router' is now used in place of the original definition of 'gateway'. Currently, a gateway is a communications device/program which passes data between networks having similar functions but dissimilar implementations. This should not be confused with a protocol converter.

geek Slang (USA). Derogatory term for computer user or enthusiast of some sort.

Gopher A distributed information service that makes available hierarchical collections of information across the Internet. Gopher uses a simple protocol that allows a single Gopher client to access information from any accessible Gopher server, providing the user with a single 'Gopher space' of information. Public domain versions of the client and server are available.

hacker A person who delights in having an intimate understanding of the internal workings of a system, computers and computer networks in particular. The term is often misused in a pejorative context, where 'cracker' would be the correct term. In the UK the terms 'hacker' and 'cracker' are used indiscriminately.

handshake Inter-device system to prevent data loss due to data overflow. 'Soft' handshaking embeds GO/STOP codes into the data stream (XON/XOFF). 'Hard' handshaking raises and lowers voltages on the communications port. More properly called frame or over-run control.

header The portion of a packet, preceding the actual data, containing source and destination addresses, and error checking and other fields. A header is also the part of an electronic mail message that precedes the body of a message and contains, among other things, the message originator, date and time.

hierarchical routing The complex problem of routing on large networks can be simplified by reducing the size of the networks. This is accomplished by breaking a network into a hierarchy of networks, where each level is responsible for its own routing. The Internet has, basically, three levels: the backbones, the mid-levels, and the stub networks. The backbones know how to route between the mid-levels, the mid-levels know how to route between the sites, and each site (being an autonomous system) knows how to route internally.

IANA See *Internet Assigned Numbers Authority.*

Integrated Services Digital Network (ISDN) An emerging technology which is beginning to be offered by the telephone carriers of the world. ISDN combines voice and digital network services in a single medium, making it possible to offer customers digital data services as well as voice connections through a single 'wire'. The standards that define ISDN are specified by CCITT.

International Telecommunications Union (ITU) Anglicization of the proper French name of the Union Internationale des Télécommunications (UIT), resident in Geneva, Switzerland. ITU is the treaty-established world centre for agreements on telecommunications technical and operating standards and is a constituent body of the United Nations, engaging also in international development and education concerning telecommunications.

internet While an internet is a network, the term 'internet' is usually used to refer to a collection of networks interconnected with routers.

Internet (note the capital 'I') The Internet is the largest internet in the world. It is a three-level hierarchy composed of backbone networks (for example, NSFNET, MILNET), mid-level networks, and stub networks. The Internet is a multiprotocol internet.

internet address An IP address that uniquely identifies a node on an internet. An Internet address (capital 'I'), uniquely identifies a node on the Internet.

Internet Assigned Numbers Authority (IANA) The central registry for various Internet protocol parameters, such as port, protocol and enterprise numbers, and options, codes and types. The currently assigned values are listed in the 'Assigned Numbers' document [STD2]. To request a number assignment, contact the IANA at *iana@isi.edu.*

Internet Protocol (IP) The Internet Protocol, defined in STD 5, RFC 791, is the network layer for the TCP/IP Protocol Suite. It is a connectionless, best-effort packet switching protocol.

Internet Relay Chat (IRC) A worldwide 'party line' protocol that allows one to converse with others in real time. IRC is structured as a network of servers, each of which accepts connections from client programs, one per user. [Source: HACKER]

IP See *Internet Protocol.*

IP address The 32-bit address defined by the Internet Protocol in STD 5, RFC 791. It is usually represented in dotted decimal notation.

IRC See *Internet Relay Chat.*

ISDN See *Integrated Services Digital Network.*

ITU See *International Telecommunications Union.*

KA9Q A popular implementation of TCP/IP and associated protocols for amateur packet radio systems.

Kermit A popular file transfer protocol developed by Columbia University. Because Kermit runs in most operating environments, it provides an easy method of file transfer. Kermit is NOT the same as FTP. [Source: MALAMUD]

LAPM Link Access Procedure for Modems. V42 also contains 'Alternative Protocol', which means that it's compatible with MNP classes 2 through 4.

leased line Any circuit or combination of circuits designated to be at the exclusive disposal of a given user. Synonyms: Private line; Full Period Line; Dedicated Line, Tie Line (colloquial).

listserv An automated mailing list distribution system originally designed for the Bitnet/EARN network.

local loop The local circuit connection between the end user and the user's nearest telephone exchange office; notorious for being the poorest, weakest link in data circuits.

mail gateway A machine that connects two or more electronic mail systems (including dissimilar mail systems) and transfers messages between them. Sometimes the mapping and translation can be quite complex, and it generally requires a store-and-forward scheme whereby the message is received from one system completely before it is transmitted to the next system, after suitable translations.

mailing list A list of email addresses, used by a mail exploder, to forward messages to groups of people. Generally, a mailing list is used to discuss a certain set of topics, and different mailing lists discuss different topics. A mailing list may be moderated. This means that messages sent to the list are actually sent to a moderator who determines whether or not to send the messages on to everyone else. Requests to subscribe to, or leave, a mailing list should ALWAYS be sent to the list's '-request' address (for example, *ietf-request@cnri.reston.va.us* for the IETF mailing list).

maximum transmission unit (MTU) The largest frame length which may be sent on a physical medium.

MIME See *Multipurpose Internet Mail Extension.*

MNP Proprietary 'standard' for modem data compression/error correction. Early non-V42 bis modems use MNP 5 for both error correction and data compression, as does some communications software. Later modems offer MNP 10. V42/V42 bis is more common.

modem Modulator/demodulator. A piece of equipment that connects a computer to a data transmission line (typically a telephone line of some sort). Modems transfer data at speeds ranging from 300 bits per second (bps) to 19.2 Kbps. 28 Kbps modems will be here Real Soon Now (RSN).

moderator A person, or small group of people, who manages moderated mailing lists and newsgroups. Moderators are responsible for determining which email submissions are passed on to the list.

MTU See *maximum transmission unit.*

MUD See *Multi-User Domain.*

Multipurpose Internet Mail Extension (MIME) An extension to Internet email which provides the ability to transfer non-textual data, such as graphics, audio and fax. It is defined in RFC 1341.

Multi-User Domain (MUD) A game available on the Internet where multiple users can take part simultaneously.

Multi-User Dungeon (MUD) Adventure Role playing games, or simulations played on the Internet. Devotees call them 'text-based virtual reality adventures'. The games can feature fantasy combat, booby traps and magic. Players interact in real time and can change the 'world' in the game as they play it. Most MUDs are based on the telnet protocol. [Source: LAQUEY]

nerd Slang (USA). See *dweeb.*

Netiquette A pun on 'etiquette' referring to proper behaviour on a network.

network A computer network is a data communications system which interconnects computer systems at various different sites. A network may be composed of any combination of LANs, MANs or WANs (Local, Metropolitan or Wide Area Networks).

network address The network portion of an IP address. For a class A network, the network address is the first byte of the IP address. For a class B network, the network address is the first two bytes of the IP address. For a class C network, the network address is the first three bytes of the IP address. In each case, the remainder is the host address. In the Internet, assigned network addresses are globally unique.

Network File System (NFS) A protocol developed by Sun Microsystems, and defined in RFC 1094, which allows a computer system to access files over a network as if they were on its local disks. This protocol has been incorporated in products by more than 200 companies, and is now a *de facto* Internet standard. [Source: NNSC]

Network News Transfer Protocol (NNTP) A protocol, defined in RFC 977, for the distribution, inquiry, retrieval and posting of news articles.

Network Time Protocol (NTP) A protocol that ensures accurate local timekeeping with reference to radio and atomic clocks located on the Internet. This protocol is capable of synchronizing distributed clocks within milliseconds over long time periods. It is defined in STD 12, RFC 1119.

NFS See *Network File System.*

NNTP See *Network News Transfer Protocol.*

NTP See *Network Time Protocol.*

Packet InterNet Groper (PING) A program used to test reachability of destinations by sending them an ICMP echo request and waiting for a reply. The term is used as a verb: 'Ping host X to see if it is up!' [Source: RFC1208]

packet switching The technique in which a stream of data is broken into standardized units called 'packets', each of which contains address, sequence, control, size and error checking information in addition to the user data. Specialized packet switches operate on this added information to move the packets to their destination in the proper sequence and again present them in a contiguous stream.

parity A constant state of equality; one of the oldest and simplest methods of error checking data transmission. Characters are forced into parity (total number of marking bits odd or even as selected by choice) by adding a one or zero bit as appropriate when transmitted; parity is then checked as odd or even at the receiver.

parity bit A check bit appended to an array of binary digits to make the sum of all the digits always odd or always even.

PEM See *Privacy Enhanced Mail.*

PING See *Packet InterNet Groper.*

Point of Presence (PoP) A site where there exists a collection of telecommunications equipment, usually digital leased lines and multi-protocol routers.

Point-to-Point Protocol (PPP) The Point-to-Point Protocol, defined in RFC 1171, provides a method for transmitting packets over serial point-to-point links.

PoP See *Point of Presence*

POP See *Post Office Protocol.*

Post Office Protocol (POP) A protocol designed to allow single-user hosts to read mail from a server. There are three versions: POP, POP2, and POP3. Later versions are NOT compatible with earlier versions.

postmaster The person responsible for taking care of electronic mail problems, answering queries about users, and other related work at a site.

PPP See *Point-to-Point Protocol.*

Privacy Enhanced Mail (PEM) Internet email which provides confidentiality, authentication and message integrity using various encryption methods.

quad standard Modem providing four CCITT modes, usually V21, V22/ V22 bis, V23.

quin standard Modem providing five CCITT modes, usually V21, V22/ V22 bis, V23, V32.

remote login Operating on a remote computer, using a protocol over a computer network, as though locally attached.

Request For Comments (RFC) The document series, begun in 1969, which describes the Internet suite of protocols and related experiments. Not all (in fact very few) RFCs describe Internet standards, but all Internet standards are written up as RFCs. The RFC series of documents is unusual in that the proposed protocols are forwarded by the Internet research and development community, acting on their own behalf, as opposed to the formally reviewed and standardized protocols that are promoted by organizations such as CCITT and ANSI.

RFC See *Request for Comments*.

router A device which forwards traffic between networks. The forwarding decision is based on network layer information and routing tables, often constructed by routing protocols. See also *gateway*.

RS-232 Short for 'Electrical Industries of America Recommended Standard number 232'. Refers to the port through which a device communicates. It is the most common technical specification for interconnection of DTEs to DCEs; extremely close equivalent to the suite of CCITT V24/V28 and ISO-2110.

Serial Line IP (SLIP) A protocol used to run IP over serial lines, such as telephone circuits or RS-232 cables, interconnecting two systems. SLIP is defined in RFC 1055.

server A provider of resources (for example, file servers and name servers).

SIG Special Interest Group. Called a forum on some systems, notably CompuServe.

signature The three or four line message at the bottom of a piece of email or a Usenet article which identifies the sender. Large signatures (over five lines) are generally frowned upon.

Simple Mail Transfer Protocol (SMTP) A protocol, defined in STD 10, RFC 821, used to transfer electronic mail between computers. It is a server-to-server protocol, so other protocols are used to access the messages.

Simple Network Management Protocol (SNMP) The Internet standard protocol, defined in STD 15, RFC 1157, developed to manage nodes on an IP network. It is currently possible to manage wiring hubs, toasters, jukeboxes, and so on.

SLIP See *Serial Line IP*.

SMTP See *Simple Mail Transfer Protocol*.

SNMP See *Simple Network Management Protocol*.

TCP See *Transmission Control Protocol*.

TCP/IP Protocol Suite Transmission Control Protocol over Internet

Protocol. This is a common shorthand which refers to the suite of transport and application protocols which runs over IP.

telnet Telnet is the Internet standard protocol for remote terminal connection service. It is defined in STD 8, RFC 854 and extended with options by many other RFCs (requests for comments).

ter Means 'third working' or third implementation, as used in CCITT recommendations.

TERBO Non CCITT-ratified proprietary mode, despite the inference.

terminal (1) A point at which information can enter or leave a communications network. (2) Any device capable of sending or receiving information over a communications channel.

terminal emulator A program that allows a computer to emulate a terminal. The workstation thus appears as a terminal to the remote host. [Source: MALAMUD]

terminal equipment Devices, apparatus and their associated interfaces used to forward information to a local customer or distant terminal.

Transmission Control Protocol (TCP) An Internet Standard transport layer protocol defined in STD 7, RFC 793.

transmission speed The maximum rate at which data may be sent through the telephone system. Actual throughput is increased by use of data compression techniques.

Trojan Horse A computer program which carries within itself a means to allow the creator of the program access to the system using it. See RFC 1135.

TTY Teletype. (1) The registered trade name for teleprinters and data terminals of the Teletype Corporation. (2) Used generically in the telecommunications industry for teleprinters or data terminals that emulate teleprinter operations.

UNIX-to-UNIX CoPy (UUCP) This was initially a program run under the UNIX operating system that allowed one UNIX system to send files to another UNIX system via dial-up phone lines. Today, the term is more commonly used to describe the large international network which uses the UUCP protocol to pass news and electronic mail.

URL Uniform Resource Locator. Standard form of textual addressing used on the World Wide Web.

Usenet A collection of thousands of topically named newsgroups, the computers that run the protocols, and the people who read and submit Usenet news. Not all Internet hosts subscribe to Usenet and not all Usenet hosts are on the Internet. See also: *Network News Transfer Protocol, UNIX-to-UNIX CoPy*. [Source: NWNET]

UUCP See *UNIX-to-UNIX CoPy*.

UUEncode Program for personal computers, which translates binary files into ASCII representations. Converted binary files can then be transferred as electronic mail. Used to get over the 7-bit limitations of the Internet. UUDecode is used to effect the reverse transformation.

V42 Error correction standard

V42 bis Standard for error correction/data compression within modems. A modem equipped with V42 bis can multiply throughput by up to four times if the data is compressible.

virus A program that replicates itself on computer systems by incorporating itself into other programs which are shared among computer systems.

W3 See *World Wide Web*.

WAIS See *Wide Area Information Servers*.

white pages The Internet supports several databases that contain basic information about users, such as email addresses, telephone numbers and postal addresses. These databases can be searched to get information about particular individuals. Because they serve a function akin to the telephone book, these databases are often referred to as 'white pages'.

whois An Internet program which allows users to query a database of people and other Internet entities, such as domains, networks and hosts, kept at the DDN NIC. The information for people shows a person's company name, address, phone number and email address. [Source: FYI4]

Wide Area Information Servers (WAIS) A distributed information service which offers simple natural language input, indexed searching for fast retrieval, and a 'relevance feedback' mechanism which allows the results of initial searches to influence future searches. Public domain implementations are available.

World Wide Web (WWW or W3) A hypertext-based, distributed information system created by researchers at CERN in Switzerland. Users may create, edit or browse hypertext documents. The clients and servers are freely available.

worm A computer program that replicates itself and is self-propagating. Worms, as opposed to viruses, are meant to spawn in network environments. Network worms were first defined by Shoch and Hupp of Xerox in *ACM Communications* (March 1982). The Internet worm of November 1988 is perhaps the most famous; it successfully propagated itself on over 6000 systems across the Internet.

WWW See *World Wide Web*.

X.400 The CCITT and ISO standard for electronic mail. It is widely used in Europe and Canada.

X.500 The CCITT and ISO standard for electronic directory services.

Yellow Pages (YP) A service used by UNIX administrators to manage databases distributed across a network.

YP See *Yellow Pages*.

References

BIG-LAN 'BIG-LAN Frequently Asked Questions Memo', BIG-LAN DIGEST V4:I8, February 14, 1992.

COMER Comer D. (1991). *Internetworking with TCP/IP: Principles, Protocols and Architecture*. Englewood Cliffs, NJ: Prentice-Hall.

FYI4 Malkin G and Marine A. (1992). FYI on Questions and Answers: Answers to Commonly asked "New Internet User" Questions. FYI 4, RFC 1325, Xylogics, SRI, May 1992.

HACKER 'THIS IS THE JARGON FILE', Version 2.9.8, January 1992.

HPCC 'Grand Challenges 1993: High Performance Computing and Communications'. Committee on Physical, Mathematical and Engineering Sciences of the Federal Coordinating Council for Science, Engineering and Technology.

LAQUEY LaQuey T. (with J. Ryer) (1992). *The Internet Companion: A Beginner's Guide to Global Networking*. Reading, MA: Addison-Wesley.

MALAMUD Malamud C. (1992). *Analyzing Sun Networks*. New York, NY: Van Nostrand Reinhold.

NNSC 'NNSC's Hypercard Tour of the Internet'.

NWNET Kochmer J. and NorthWestNet (1992). *The Internet Passport: NorthWestNet's Guide to Our World Online*. Bellevue, WA: NorthWestNet.

RFC1208 Jacobsen O. and Lynch D. (1991). *A Glossary of Networking Terms*. RFC 1208, Interop, Inc., March.

STD1 Postel J. (1992). *IAB Official Protocol Standards*. STD 1, RFC 1360, Internet Architecture Board, September.

STD2 Reynolds J. and Postel J. (1992). *Assigned Numbers*. STD 2, RFC 1340, USC/Information Sciences Institute, July.

TAN Tanenbaum A. (1989). *Computer Networks* 2nd edn. Englewood Cliffs, NJ: Prentice-Hall.

ZEN Kehoe B. (1992). Zen and the Art of the Internet.

Index